Grades **1–5**

**Get the GRADE!**
AQA GCSE English
**LANGUAGE**

**RESULT!**

**Authors:**
Keith Brindle
Steve Eddy
Sarah Forrest
Robert Francis
Harmeet Matharu

**Series Editor:**
**KEITH BRINDLE**

**HODDER**
EDUCATION
AN HACHETTE UK COMPANY

Photo credits and acknowledgements can be found on pages 188–189.

Although every effort has been made to ensure that website addresses are correct at time of going to press, Hodder Education cannot be held responsible for the content of any website mentioned. It is sometimes possible to find a relocated web page by typing in the address of the home page for a website in the URL window of your browser.

Orders: please contact Bookpoint Ltd, 130 Milton Park, Abingdon, Oxon OX14 4SB. Telephone: (44) 01235 827720. Fax: (44) 01235 400454. Lines are open 9.00–17.00, Monday to Saturday, with a 24-hour message answering service. Visit our website at www.hoddereducation.co.uk

© Keith Brindle, Steve Eddy, Rob Francis, Sarah Forrest, Harmeet Matharu, 2015

First published in 2015 by

Hodder Education

An Hachette UK Company,

338 Euston Road

London NW1 3BH

Impression number 5 4 3 2 1
Year 2019 2018 2017 2016 2015

Cover artwork by Jacquie Boyd at Début Art Limited

Illustrations by Barking Dog Art, Oxford Designers and Illustrators

Design and layouts by Lorraine Inglis

Printed in Italy

A catalogue record for this title is available from the British Library

ISBN 9781471832048

# CONTENTS

# Series Editor introduction

## About this book

Welcome to Hodder Education's *Get the Grade! for AQA GCSE English Language*.

This book will guide you, stage by stage, through the different parts of the AQA GCSE English Language examination. It offers you the knowledge that you need to succeed and the practices that will develop your skills and improve your performance. The aim is to lift you up to the vital Grade 5 level, but to make it a really pleasant journey: we hope you will enjoy the texts and the activities so that learning about how to do well in the exam can be a truly positive experience.

The texts and activities have been selected so that they are appropriate for this level of work. They are demanding but are intended to build your confidence, and you will be supported through each phase. Everyone should be able to do what is being asked of them and make progress – and with a smile on their face.

Throughout, this book gives you vital information. As well as dealing with all the questions you will encounter, offering advice on how to tackle them and activities to prepare you for your Big Day, it also provides regular Examiner Comments, so that you are aware of how examiners think and what they expect; and it also shows you graded work, letting you see exactly what you need to do to improve your marks and what is needed to lift you to a higher level.

Everything is presented in a step-by-step way, which allows you to work independently or with the help of a teacher.

## How this book is organised

The book is divided into three main sections:

Units 1–5 are on Paper 1, Section A: Reading fiction texts

Units 6–9 are on Paper 2, Section A: Reading non-fiction texts

Units 10–17 are on Section B (both papers):
- Improving the quality of your writing
- Writing to describe, narrate and offer a point of view.

There are **regular features**, which you will encounter throughout the book:

- The skills are divided into sensible sections within the units.
- 'What this unit involves' tells you about the skills you will be developing within the unit.
- 'Practising for success' helps you develop the skills you need.
- 'Examiner comments' tell you exactly what the examiner is looking for.
- 'Assessment comments' show why grades have been awarded.
- 'Key terms' home in on the terminology that will get you better marks.
- 'Boost your grade' is a section helping you to improve your final grade.
- 'Test yourself' gives a final activity so you can see how much you have learnt in the unit.

## The Series Editor

Keith Brindle has been a Principal Examiner for four AQA English examinations. He was a Head of English for fifteen years and has written over fifty English books. He works in schools across the country, helping GCSE students improve their examination skills.

Keith Brindle

Good luck with your English Language work and in the exam itself!

# About the examination...

## The exam papers

You will have to complete two examination papers.
Each lasts for 1 hour and 45 minutes.

### Paper 1

**Section A:** there will be four questions based on an extract from a modern novel: one hour.

**Section B:** you will be offered a choice of essay questions, but will have to write to describe or to narrate (tell a story): 45 minutes.

### Paper 2

**Section A:** again there will be four questions, but in this case they will be based on two non-fiction texts. One of the texts will be from the nineteenth century: one hour.

**Section B:** there will be just one question, asking you to give your point of view on a given topic: 45 minutes.

## What is expected of you

Across the Section As, you will be tested on your ability to:
- find information and link evidence from different texts
- comment on how writers use language and structure for effect
- use subject terminology to support your views
- compare writers' ideas and how they present them
- judge texts critically and support what you say with evidence from the texts.

In the Section Bs, you will be tested on your ability to:
- communicate clearly and effectively
- write appropriately for purpose and audience
- organise your writing effectively
- use a range of vocabulary and sentence structures
- spell and punctuate accurately.

# Paper 1, Section A

## What you have to do…

The AQA examination papers are very predictable, so it is much easier for you to prepare and then to perform well on the day.

Paper 1, Section A has four questions about an extract from a novel written in the 20th or 21st century. There are 40 marks available.

You need to take about an hour on this section. You must be prepared to spend up to 15 minutes reading the source carefully, then 45 minutes or more answering the four questions on it.

The questions will be as follows:

| Q1 | 4 marks | You will have to find four details in the source and list them. |
|----|---------|---|
| Q2 | 8 marks | This is the language question. You will be asked how the writer uses language for a particular purpose. |
| Q3 | 8 marks | This question is on the structure of the source: how the writer has organised the writing. |
| Q4 | 20 marks | This question will ask you how the writer has created a particular impression – of the characters, or the setting or whatever – and how you feel about what you have read. |

Question 1 is slightly different, but in each of the other questions you will be expected to make points, support them with evidence from the source and explain your ideas.

There are no marks for spelling, sentence construction or punctuation on this section, but the more clearly you can express yourself, the easier it is for the examiner to understand and reward your efforts.

# Using evidence to support your ideas

**What this unit involves**

**In this unit you will learn how to:**
⇨ find relevant points for your answers
⇨ use quotations
⇨ embed quotations.

**What this unit involves**

This unit deals with how to use quotations and material from the source text to help illustrate what you are trying to say.

When you are answering questions on a passage in the examination you will need to refer to the source text to be successful.

## 1 Selecting the right evidence

When you write your answers to most of the questions in Section A of the examination, you will need to select evidence to support your ideas. This will show the examiner that you have properly understood the passage.

### Practising for success

Read this extract from a short story about a young boy who wants to prove himself to some older boys by being able to swim through a long tunnel into the sea. He must be able to hold his breath for well over two minutes to do this. There is a crack in the rock above him but there is only more water above it.

He was at the end of what he could do. He looked up at the crack as if it were filled with air and not water, as if he could put his mouth to it to draw in air. A hundred and fifteen, he heard himself say inside his head—but he had said that long ago. He must go on into the blackness ahead, or he would drown. His head was swelling, his lungs cracking. A hundred and fifteen, a hundred and fifteen pounded through his head, and he feebly clutched at rocks in the dark, pulling himself forward, leaving the brief space of sunlit water behind. He felt he was dying. He was no longer conscious. He struggled on in the darkness between lapses into unconsciousness. An immense, swelling pain filled his head, and then darkness cracked with an explosion of green light. His hands, groping forward, met nothing; and his feet, kicking back, propelled him out into the open sea.

Doris Lessing, *Through the Tunnel* (1955)

## ACTIVITY 1

**1** What does the writer tell us about the change in the light?

Idea is picked out

**Quotation** is used to support the idea

> The writer shows how suddenly darkness became light again by saying: 'darkness cracked with an explosion of green light'. The idea of an 'explosion' of light shows that it was not only sudden but almost violent.

Explanation of the effect of the idea is given

The writer is able to create tension and excitement in this passage. We wonder if the boy will die, or if he will succeed.

**2** Select three words or phrases that show that this is a potentially life-threatening experience.

| WORD OR PHRASE | WHAT IT MAKES YOU THINK |
|---|---|
| He felt like he was dying | It sounds as if there is no hope |
|  |  |
|  |  |

If you were asked to write about how tension is created in this passage, a successful answer would not just retell what happens but would pick out supporting examples – like those you have just found – and explain them.

### Key term

**A quotation** is material taken from a source. Use speech marks around it to show you have taken it from the source.

### Examiner comment

A useful technique to help you get more marks is **PEE**.

- make a **p**oint
- give some **e**vidence
- offer an **e**xplanation.

Only select material that supports your point. Using randomly selected quotations will not help you answer a question and will show an examiner that you have not understood a passage very well.

3

**3** Look at the following student responses to the question 'How does the writer create tension in the passage?'

## Student A

He repeats things which shows that he is starting to become unwell and doesn't know if he will get out. There are some short sentences and some lists of what he does. He is in pain and it is hurting him to be under the water this long.

(Grade 2)

## Student B

Tension is created by showing that the boy had counted to over 115 and was still in the water. This is repeated which shows he is desperate to get out and not sure quite how long he has been under the water. He feels like he is dying which shows that he is not sure he will survive.

(Grade 3)

## Student C

The writer uses several techniques to build up tension in the passage. 'A hundred and fifteen' is repeated several times, which shows what a long time he has been under the water and he is becoming desperate to get out. Lessing also says he suffers from 'an immense swelling pain' which shows that he is close to losing consciousness and he is feeling very unwell.

(Grade 5)

Look at how the ideas included in these answers have been supported. Higher grade answers will not only identify techniques, but also offer evidence and comment on the evidence presented.

**4** Why might these grades have been awarded?

Read the following description of Paul Wentworth.

**Zoe**

Hi. I'm Zoe. Zoe May Askew. Or Zoe may not (Joke!). I'm fourteen. My friend at school is Tabitha. Tabitha Flinders Wentworth for short. She's fourteen too. If the name seems familiar to you it's no big surprise. Her dad's Paul Wentworth of Wentworth and Lodge Developments (PLC), the outfit that shoved up practically every residential estate in practically every suburb in England. You're bound to have seen their boards, plus their ads on TV. He's into about a million other things too, Tabby says. Security. Roads. Power. He's into power all right. Chair of the Suburb Select-men, Chair of Schools Management Committee, etcetera, etcetera, etcetera. Dog leaves a mess on the sidewalk, Paul Wentworth'll make himself chair of it.

Robert Swindells, *Daz 4 Zoe* (1995)

Wentworth & Lodge
Developments (PLC)

**5** Pick out three quotations from the source that make it sound as if Zoe does not like Paul Wentworth.

Consider this response:

General point on Paul Wentworth's company and how it is described

The writer shows her dislike for Paul Wentworth by describing his company in negative terms: 'the outfit that shoved up practically every suburb in England.'
    The words 'shoved up' make it sound as if very little care has been taken building the houses and that they were done almost forcefully.
    Zoe makes him seem power-crazy, which is not a good thing.
    'He's into power all right.'
    The words 'all right' are quite conversational, but make it seem as if she is laughing at the thought of how much power he likes – there is no doubt he likes power.

Evidence picked out to support this

Explanations of the quotation and the effect of the language

Point

Supporting evidence

Explanations of the quotation and the effect

This answer has Grade 5 quality. Notice, particularly, that the final sentence moves beyond simple explanation: *'The words 'all right' are … but make it seem as if … there is no doubt …'*

Several points are being made, which is a sign of analysis – a higher order skill.

**Examiner comment**

To reach Grade 5, try to use **PEA**: **p**oint, **e**vidence, **a**nalysis.

5

**6** Use quotations from the source to continue the **analysis** of the 'Zoe' passage.

> ## Key terms
>
> **Analysis**: when more than one explanation is offered, or ideas are joined up and extended.
>
> **Embedded quotation:** this means that you would use a few words or just one word, in quotation marks, within the flow of your sentence.

### Boost your grade ⬆

When writing a response about a passage it is impressive if you can pick out short quotations and use them in an **embedded** form in your answer.

For example, consider this passage about a lighthouse:

> Out there, in the cold water, far from land, we waited every night for the coming of the fog, and it came, and we oiled the brass machinery and lit the fog light up in the stone tower.  Feeling like two birds in the grey sky, McDunn and I sent the light touching out, red, then white, and then red again, to guide the lonely ships.
>
> Ray Bradbury, *The Fog Horn* (1974)

If you were writing about the men, you might say something like:

> The writer describes the men as 'feeling like two birds it the sky', meaning that they were high up and above the rest of the world – perhaps feeling free.

The quotations are embedded as they flow naturally into the sentence and it all makes grammatical sense. Notice how one quotation is just one word long and another is only five words long.

Write a description of the place, embedding quotations in your answer.

## Test yourself

Read the following passage:

Everyone called him Pop Eye. Even in those days, when I was a skinny thirteen-year-old, I thought he probably knew about his nickname but didn't care. His eyes were too interested in what lay up ahead to notice us barefoot kids.

He looked like someone who had seen or known great suffering and hadn't been able to forget it. His large eyes in his large head stuck out further than anyone else's—like they wanted to leave the surface of his face. They made you think of someone who can't get out of the house quickly enough.

Pop Eye wore the same white linen suit every day. His trousers snagged on his bony knees in the sloppy heat. Some days he wore a clown's nose. His nose was already big. He didn't need that red lightbulb. But for reasons we couldn't think of he wore the red nose on certain days—which may have meant something to him. We never saw him smile. And on those days he wore the clown's nose you found yourself looking away because you never saw such sadness.

Lloyd Jones, *Mister Pip* (2008)

1 Pick out three short quotations from the source that show that Pop Eye has had bad luck.
2 Put these quotations into a paragraph or two about the passage, answering the question:
How does the writer make you think that Pop Eye is someone who has had a difficult life so far?

### What you have learned !

In this unit you have learned how to:
● pick out relevant evidence from the source
● select and use quotations
● embed quotations.

# Q1 Finding relevant details

## What this unit involves

This unit deals with Paper 1, Question 1. You will have to read a passage of fiction and answer a question which will ask you to select four details from the opening of the source and write them down.

There are 4 marks for this question so you should spend no more than about 4 or 5 minutes on it.

## 1 Looking for relevant evidence

When answering the first simple question it is important that you:
- read the source carefully
- consider the question
- go back to the source and this time underline details that seem to answer the question
- select the details you intend to use, then write down your answers.

## Practising for success

Read the following source written by a football supporter.

> I have learned things from the game. Much of my knowledge of locations in Britain and Europe comes not from school, but from away games or the sports pages, and hooliganism has given me both a taste for **sociology** and **a degree of fieldwork experience**. I have learned the value of investing time and emotion in things I cannot control, and of belonging to a community whose **aspirations** I share completely and uncritically. And on my first visit to **Selhurst Park** with my friend Frog, I saw a dead body, still my first, and learned a little bit about, well, life itself.
>
> Nick Hornby, *Fever Pitch* (2010)

**sociology** is a study of how people behave

**a degree of fieldwork experience** means a certain amount of first-hand knowledge

**aspirations** are hopes or ambitions

**Selhurst Park** is Crystal Palace's football ground

## ACTIVITY 1

**1** List four things that the narrator says he has learned in this extract.

**Student answer**

> 1 About belonging to a community
>
> 2 Sociology
>
> 3 Value of investing time and emotion in things he can't control
>
> 4 Things about himself

**Examiner comment**

In the exam it is helpful to underline the key words in the question. This will help you focus on what you should be writing in your answer.

All of these answers are correct. It is acceptable to write direct quotations and one-word answers, where appropriate, from the source when answering a question of this kind. You will also be rewarded if you put the ideas into your own words – but that is not necessary.

**Discussion point**

**2** Look at this extract from later in the same chapter. It is about Highbury, where Arsenal used to play.

Choose four reasons the writer gives for having his ashes scattered across the Highbury pitch.

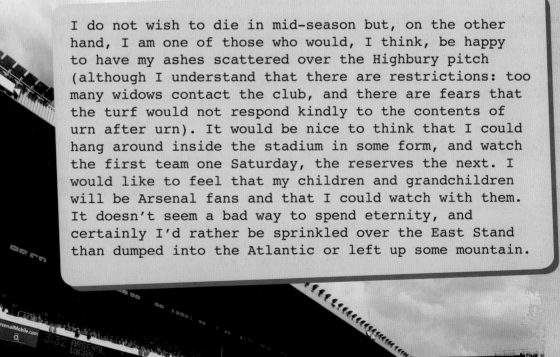

> I do not wish to die in mid-season but, on the other hand, I am one of those who would, I think, be happy to have my ashes scattered over the Highbury pitch (although I understand that there are restrictions: too many widows contact the club, and there are fears that the turf would not respond kindly to the contents of urn after urn). It would be nice to think that I could hang around inside the stadium in some form, and watch the first team one Saturday, the reserves the next. I would like to feel that my children and grandchildren will be Arsenal fans and that I could watch with them. It doesn't seem a bad way to spend eternity, and certainly I'd rather be sprinkled over the East Stand than dumped into the Atlantic or left up some mountain.

# 2 Selecting the correct information

Sometimes students pick out information from the wrong part of the source and, as a result, lose marks. The material you will need in order to answer the first question will be from the opening section of the source.

### ACTIVITY 1

Read the source below, taken from *Things Fall Apart* by Chinua Achebe.

Okonkwo was well known throughout the nine villages and even beyond. His fame rested on solid personal achievements. As a young man of eighteen he had brought honour to his village by throwing Amalinze the Cat. Amalinze was the great wrestler who for seven years was unbeaten, from Umuofia to Mbaino. He was called the Cat
5 because his back would never touch the earth. It was this man that Okonkwo threw in a fight which the old men agreed was one of the fiercest since the founder of their
7 town engaged a spirit of the wild for seven days and seven nights.

The drums beat and the flutes sang and the spectators held their breath. Amalinze was a wily craftsman, but Okonkwo was as slippery as a fish in water. Every nerve
10 and every muscle stood out on their arms, on their backs and their thighs, and one almost heard them stretching to breaking point. In the end Okonkwo threw the Cat. That was many years ago, twenty years or more, and during this time Okonkwo's fame had grown like a bush-fire in the **harmattan**. He was tall and huge, and his bushy eyebrows and wide nose gave him a very severe look. He breathed heavily, and
15 it was said that, when he slept, his wives and children in their out-houses could hear him breathe. When he walked, his heels hardly touched the ground and he seemed to walk on springs, as if he was going to pounce on somebody. And he did pounce on people quite often. He had a slight stammer and whenever he was angry and could not get his words out quickly enough, he would use his fists. He had no
20 patience with unsuccessful men. He had had no patience with his father.

{ **harmattan** is a dry and dusty African wind }

Chinua Achebe, *Things Fall Apart* (1958)

**1 a)** List four things you learn about Okonkwo in lines 1–7.
   **b)** If you had been asked to find things from lines 1–20 what else could you add to your list?

If you had selected anything from the second paragraph to answer Question 1a, it would not have gained you a mark in the examination.

Read the extract below from Robert Swindells' novel *Stone Cold*.

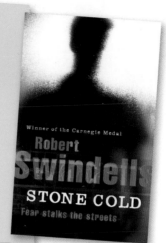

We were a happy family, you know – as happy as most, till Dad ran off with a receptionist in 1991, when I was fourteen and at the local comp. This mucked up my school work for quite a while, but that's not why I ended up like this. No. Vincent's to blame for that. Good old Vince. Mum's boyfriend. You should see him. I mean, Mum's no Kylie Minogue – but Vincent. He's about fifty for a start, and he's one of these old dudes that wear cool gear and try to act young and it doesn't work because they've got grey hair and fat bellies and they just make themselves pathetic. And as if that's not enough, Vince likes his ale. You should see the state Vincent's in when he and Mum come home from the club. He's got this very loud laugh – laughing at nothing, if you know what I mean – and he stands with his arm around Mum, slurring his words as he tells me to call him Dad.

Robert Swindells, *Stone Cold* (1993)

**2** Question: List four negative things the narrator says about Vince. This is a student's response.

**3** Which answer is incorrect and why?

Read this extract, then answer the question.
**1** Write a list of four ways the narrator tries to encourage Richard Parker to stay alive.

The ship sank. It made a sound like a monstrous metallic burp. Things bubbled at the surface and then vanished. Everything was screaming: the sea, the wind, my heart. From the lifeboat I saw something in the water.

I cried, "Richard Parker, is that you? It's so hard to see. Oh, that this rain would stop! Richard Parker? Richard Parker? Yes, it is you!"

I could see his head. He was struggling to stay at the surface of the water.

"Jesus, Mary, Muhammad and Vishnu, how good to see you, Richard Parker! Don't give up, please. Come to the lifeboat. Do you hear this whistle? **TREEEEEE! TREEEEEE!**

TREEEEEE! is the sound of a whistle being blown

**11**

> TREEEEEE! You heard right. Swim, swim! You're a strong swimmer. It's not a hundred feet."
>
> He had seen me. He looked panic-stricken. He started swimming my way. The water about him was shifting wildly. He looked small and helpless.
>
> "What are you doing, Richard Parker? Don't you love life? Keep swimming then! TREEEEEE! TREEEEEE! TREEEEEE! Kick with your legs. Kick! Kick! Kick!"
>
> He stirred in the water and made to swim.
>
> Yann Martel, *Life of Pi* (2001)

**2** Read **Student Response A** below. Have you put the same things? What are the differences?

## Student Response A

This quotation is relevant to the question and would be awarded a mark

1 Kick! Kick! Kick!

This is about Richard Parker and not the narrator and is therefore not the correct information

2 He looked panic-stricken

3 He swam towards him

This is also about Richard Parker and not the narrator and so not correct

4 He blew a whistle

This is correct and an appropriate answer

**3** Next, look at **Student Response B** and write down four annotations like those for **Student Response A**.

## Student Response B

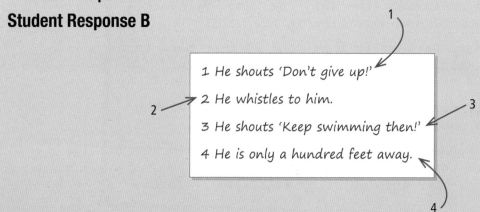

1 He shouts 'Don't give up!'

2 He whistles to him.

3 He shouts 'Keep swimming then!'

4 He is only a hundred feet away.

## Test yourself

Read the passage below, and answer the exam question that follows. The passage is from the novel *War Horse* by Michael Morpugo.

The opening of the novel is written from the point of view of a young horse taken to be sold at auction.

My earliest memories are a confusion of hilly fields and dark, damp stables, and rats that scampered along the beams above my head. But I remember well enough the day of the horse sale. The terror of it stayed with me all my life.

I was not yet six months old, a gangling, leggy colt who had never been further than a few feet from his mother. We were parted that day in the terrible hubbub of the auction ring and I was never to see her again. She was a fine working farm horse, getting on in years but with all the strength and stamina of an Irish draught horse quite evident in her fore and hind quarters. She was sold within minutes, and before I could follow her through the gates, she was whisked out of the ring and away. But somehow I was more difficult to dispose of. Perhaps it was the wild look in my eye as I circled the ring in a desperate search for my mother, or perhaps it was that none of the farmers and gypsies there were looking for a spindly-looking half-thoroughbred colt. But whatever the reason they were a long time haggling over how little I was worth before I heard the hammer go down and I was driven out through the gates and into a pen outside.

Michael Morpugo, *War Horse* (1982)

List four things about the young horse's appearance that explain why it took a long time to sell.

### What you have learned

In this unit you have learned:
- the importance of reading the question carefully
- the importance of choosing the right material
- how to select information.

# Q2 Writing about language in literature

**In this unit you will learn to write about:**
 language techniques
 the way writers use language.

## What this unit involves

This unit deals with Paper 1, Question 2. You will have to:
- explain how writers use language to achieve effects
- support what you say with relevant vocabulary.

There are 8 marks for this question and you will have 8 or 9 minutes to answer it in the examination.

## 1 How writers use adjectives, verbs and adverbs for effect

### Key terms

**Adjectives** describe objects or places – the *magnificent* palace; the *fabulous* team.

**Verbs** a doing word – he *ran* outside; she *played* the game.

**Adverbs** describe actions – they moved *rapidly*; the team *successfully* defended their title.

---

**crescendo** means a gradual increase

**vantage point** is a place with a good view

**impenetrable** means 'can't get through'

### Practising for success

Read this description of a scene in World War I. The soldiers lived in trenches, and between the two sides was No Man's Land, where the enemy could see you and shoot at you. Horses were still used in this war.

Here, the horse telling the story has strayed into No Man's Land.

From both sides of me I heard a gradual **crescendo** of excitement and laughter rippling along the trenches, interspersed with barked orders that everyone was to keep their heads down and no one was to shoot. From my **vantage point** on the mound I could see only an occasional glimpse of a steel helmet, my only evidence that the voices I was hearing did indeed belong to real people. There was the sweet smell of cooking food wafting towards me and I lifted my nose to savour it. It was sweeter than the sweetest branmash I had ever tasted and it had a tinge of salt about it. I was drawn first one way and then the other by this promise of warm food, but each time I neared the trenches on either side I met an **impenetrable** barrier of loosely coiled barbed wire. The soldiers cheered me on as I came closer, showing their heads fully now over the trenches and beckoning me towards them; and when I had to turn back at the

> wire and crossed no man's land to the other side, I
> was welcomed again there by a chorus of whistling and
> clapping, but again I could find no way through the
> wire. I must have criss-crossed no man's land for much
> of that morning, and found at long last in the middle
> of this blasted wilderness a small patch of coarse,
> dank grass growing on the lip of an old crater.
>
> Michael Morpugo, *War Horse* (1982)

## ACTIVITY 1

1  When good writers describe somewhere they try and give as much information
   as possible so that the reader can see clearly the scene they are describing.
   Often they describe using their senses. Find adjectives or adverbs that the writer
   uses to describe the scene. Copy and complete a table like the one below.

| SENSE | EXAMPLE | EFFECT OF ADJECTIVE OR ADVERB |
|---|---|---|
| Sight | 'blasted wilderness' | 'blasted' is an adjective which makes it seem horrible and as if it has been destroyed by the firing of the guns ('blasted') |
| Sound | | |
| Smell | | |
| Taste | | |
| Touch | | |

**Key term**

**emotive language:** produces a strong emotional response in the reader.

Writers sometimes use a group of descriptive words to help create a scene and to build an effect.

For example, they might try to build a happy scene by describing a place using positive **emotive language** such as:

> The hills smiled in the sun, gleaming and shining under its warm rays. Between the rolling mounds of earth lay lazy valleys, glittering peacefully. Meadows, hills, grasses, bubbling brooks gathered together in perfect harmony, celebrating the beauty of the earth.

The writer, by using words such as 'gleaming', 'shining', 'glittering' and 'harmony' together, gives a real sense of somewhere valuable, like a collection of glittering jewels, which shows the perfection and value of nature.

**2 a)** Look at the words the writer uses to describe the place in the extract from *War Horse* (on pages 14–15). Pick out five words or phrases that suggest a positive feeling.

**b)** Explain how each of your chosen words or phrases makes the atmosphere seem positive.

The comment below is a useful guide to show you how this can be achieved.

| WORDS | HOW DOES THIS MAKE THE PLACE SEEM HAPPY |
|---|---|
| 'gradual crescendo of excitement and laughter' | Crescendo means getting louder, so the excitement and laughter is increasing, which shows the men are happy and joking, which gives the impression of a happy place. It shows the comradeship of the men. |
| | |

**3** While the place is happy, what makes you think there could be something dangerous there as well? How does the writer use language to create this sense?

Find the details and explain them.

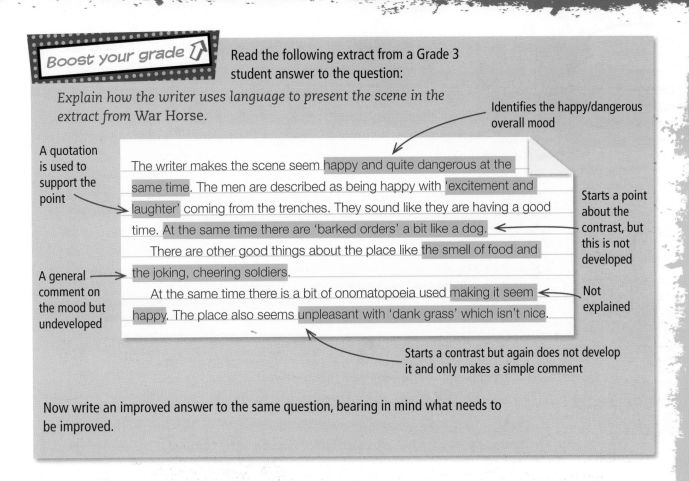

*Boost your grade* 🔼

Read the following extract from a Grade 3 student answer to the question:

*Explain how the writer uses language to present the scene in the extract from War Horse.*

A quotation is used to support the point

Identifies the happy/dangerous overall mood

The writer makes the scene seem happy and quite dangerous at the same time. The men are described as being happy with 'excitement and laughter' coming from the trenches. They sound like they are having a good time. At the same time there are 'barked orders' a bit like a dog.

There are other good things about the place like the smell of food and the joking, cheering soldiers.

A general comment on the mood but undeveloped

At the same time there is a bit of onomatopoeia used making it seem happy. The place also seems unpleasant with 'dank grass' which isn't nice.

Starts a point about the contrast, but this is not developed

Not explained

Starts a contrast but again does not develop it and only makes a simple comment

Now write an improved answer to the same question, bearing in mind what needs to be improved.

# 2 Looking at how writers use imagery to create effects

Imagery is when a writer uses descriptive language such as **similes**, **metaphors** and **personification** to create an effect. These clarify an emotion, add more detail or help the reader to imagine a place. You will get credit for identifying and explaining the use of these techniques in the examination.

## Practising for success

### Similes

### ACTIVITY 1

**1** What is being suggested by the following similes? The first one has an explanation – write one for each of the next three examples.
  **a)** The volcano was as hot as hell.

> The simile 'as hot as hell' takes the image of hell, a place we know to be very hot as a punishment for those who have sinned, and emphasises how hot the volcano is. It is like the volcano is the hottest thing there could ever be. It is so hot it seems evil, like hell itself.

*Key terms*

**Simile:** a phrase that compares one thing to another using the words 'as' or 'like', for example 'It was as cold as ice', 'She looked like a princess'.

**Metaphor:** something not literally true, for example 'My head is exploding', 'You are a pig'.

**Personification:** giving something that is not human the characteristics of a person, for example 'The sun smiled down on them'.

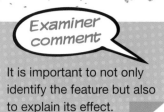

**b)** The hills rolled up and down like a ship on the stormy sea.

**c)** The dark room looked like a coffin.

**d)** The park was as quiet as the moon.

In the following extract from *Brother in the Land* by Robert Swindells, the writer uses a simile to describe the moment a nuclear bomb explodes.

> There was this sudden hot blast. It drove rain in through the doorway and spattered it on my arms and neck; warm rain. I opened my eyes. The place was flooded with bright, dusty light which flickered and began to fade as I watched. My ear was pressed to the ground and I could hear rumbling way down, like dragons in a cave; receding, growing more faint as the dragons went deeper, till you couldn't hear them at all. The light dimmed and there was only silence, and a pinkish glow with dust in it.
>
> Robert Swindells, *Brother in the Land* (1984)

**2 a)** Which part of this is the simile?

**b)** What do you think he might be describing in this simile?

**c)** What is the effect of the simile?

Read the following extract.

> The sky was the colour of Monica's sick.
>
> Of course, to understand that, you would have had to have been out with Monica the night before and seen what she had vomited over Jack's shoes, but if you know she had just eaten a chicken Balti, you will have the idea.
>
> The clouds were evil coloured, and as night fell they parted and the night gazed down like a cold and senseless void.

**scudding** means moving fast, in a straight line, driven by the wind

**3** Look at the **simile** from this passage.

> the night gazed down like a cold and senseless void

The writer is describing nightfall.

By describing it 'gazing down' it is almost as if night is looking through the evil clouds with no real concern.

**a)** What else can you tell about the coming of night from this simile? What is suggested by the fact that it is like a 'void'?

**b)** What is the effect of the writer describing the night as being 'cold and senseless'?

## Metaphors

### ACTIVITY 2

Look at the following example of a **metaphor** and the student response that follows.

> My bedroom is a rubbish dump

The idea here is that the bedroom is so untidy it looks exactly the same as a rubbish dump. In your mind you can imagine mess everywhere, such as clothes lying on the floor, the chairs, the bed and CDs, books, magazines, toiletries and discarded bits of rubbish dotted about everywhere. The writer is saying that because of the mess and the chaos, with all the person's things everywhere this room is a tip.

(Grade 5)

**1** Why is this a good explanation?

Now look at the following metaphors.

> Her bag was a car crash.

> The ball was a missile, which rocketed from one player to another before firing into the net.

**2** Write a brief summary of what you think the writer is trying to say about the bag and the ball in these examples.

Read the following extract. This is about a hot air balloon, which has been flying above a picnicking couple, and is beginning to have difficulties: one of the passengers is trying to get out.

> What we saw when we stood from our picnic was this: a huge grey balloon, the size of a house, the shape of a tear drop, had come down in the field. The pilot must have been half way out of the passenger basket as it touched the ground. His leg had become entangled in a rope that was attached to an anchor.
>
> Ian McEwan, *Enduring Love* (1997)

*Discussion point*

**3** What is the effect of comparing the balloon to a tear drop? Think about what picture the writer is trying to create in your mind and also about what the writer might be trying to prepare the reader for later in the story.

## Personification

### ACTIVITY 3

Read this passage.

> He lay remembering the last time he'd gone surfing with Quinn. Day after Halloween. It had only been early-November sun, but in memory it was very bright, every rock and pebble and sand crab outlined in gold. In his memory the waves were wondrous, almost living things, blue and green and white, calling to him, challenging him to leave his worries behind and come out and play.
>
> Michael Grant, *Gone* (2009)

Now read the annotated Grade 5 student answer to the question:
**What is the effect of comparing the waves with something human?**

Identifies personification

Gives a quotation to illustrate it

Develops the explanation: begins to analyse (PEA)

Explains effect

> Because there is personification, the waves seem like something human, 'calling to him'. He enjoys surfing a lot it seems and it is as if the waves are friends calling him out to come in and play with them. He loves the idea of being able to go out and have fun, just as you would do if you were going out with your friends.

Next, read the following passage.

> It was so easy to feel at home there. The house held out its arms to me and seemed to kiss me on the cheek as I entered and the family treated me as if I belonged. They gave me a diary and it was my friend too. I told it my secrets and it kept them safe. Suddenly, and for the first time in my life, I was happy and I was not alone.

**1** How is personification used to create a mood here? Write an explanation like the Grade 5 one above.

**Boost your grade**

In this extract, Jess has just started a relationship with Fred and he has managed to buy tickets for a music festival. However, her mother's plans look set to ruin everything.

> Disaster! Jess tried to hide her horror. Her mum frowned. "What's wrong sweetheart? It's what you've always wanted. A trip to see your Dad! I rang him about it last night and he can't wait to see you! And there'll be sun, sea, art and ice-cream! Plus lots of interesting places on the way down there. It's the holiday of a lifetime. For goodness' sake, Jess, what's the matter?"

Jess could not possibly, ever, tell. She would rather run through the supermarket stark naked and farting than reveal her secret to Mum. This sudden fabulous surprise holiday was going to ruin her life, big time. Jess's heart sank and sank and sank until it was right down on the carpet like a very ill pet.

But she must try and sound delighted. "Nothing's wrong. I've just got a bit of a headache. But hey Mum! Thanks! It'll be fantastic! When do we leave?" She tried desperately to force a bit of enthusiasm into her voice, but it was hopeless — like trying to cram her bum into size ten jeans.

"We'll set off the day after tomorrow," said her Mum, with the excited smile of a practised torturer. "Early. There won't be so much traffic then, and we can just potter gently down into the countryside. Oh I can't wait! It's going to be marvellous!"

Mum's eyes glazed over and she stared out of the window with a look of faraway rapture, as if the angel of the Lord had just appeared over Tesco's. "Ruined abbeys!" she drooled. "Rare wildflowers! Bronze Age burial mounds!"

Sue Limb, *Girl (Nearly 16) Absolute Torture* (2010)

Select five examples of language being used for effect and say why the writer has used them.

Examiner comment

For the best marks you should explain in detail the effects that language creates for the reader.

This is an extract from a Grade 5 analysis:

*Overview given and identifies similes are being used here*

The writer uses a few similes to humorously show Jess's feelings that the trip her mother has organised is an absolute disaster for her. The first one is 'Jess's heart sank and sank and sank until it was right down on the carpet like a very ill pet.' This is funny as it sounds as though her heart is getting lower and lower until it is on the ground. Making it seem like a very ill pet makes it sound as though her heart is something to love, but also something that is almost pathetic. The next amusing simile is where she describes it all being hopeless 'like trying to cram her bum into size ten jeans.' In other words, there is no way she is getting into those jeans, just as she will never work up any enthusiasm. The cramming idea is also one that many girls will understand.

*Quotation used in support*

*Explanation of the effect of the simile*

*Development of explanation*

*Another simile identified*

*Quotation used to support the point*

*Analysis of the effect*

Compare this answer with your own. Is yours as good? If not, how could you improve it?

# 3 Writers' use of onomatopoeia and alliteration

Examples of both onomatopoeia and alliteration are likely to crop up in your examination text. As with the techniques already covered, if you can write about the effect they have on the reader, you will be rewarded.

## Practising for success

### Onomatopoeia

ACTIVITY 1

1 What words are examples of onomatopoeia in the sentences below and what effect do they create?
- They sat and listened to the ticking of the clock.
- The lion roared.
- The fireworks whizzed and screamed.
- The fire crackled.

Read the following short description.

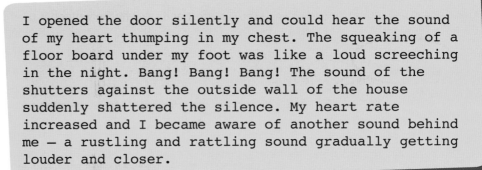

I opened the door silently and could hear the sound of my heart thumping in my chest. The squeaking of a floor board under my foot was like a loud screeching in the night. Bang! Bang! Bang! The sound of the shutters against the outside wall of the house suddenly shattered the silence. My heart rate increased and I became aware of another sound behind me — a rustling and rattling sound gradually getting louder and closer.

2 The writer uses a number of examples of onomatopoeia here.

Copy the table below and add three other examples of onomatopoeia in the description, saying what effect they create.

| EXAMPLE | EXPLANATION |
| --- | --- |
| thumping | This is a loud sound, almost violent, showing how hard the narrator's heart is beating. |
| | |
| | |
| | |

Spotting examples of onomatopoeia and explaining their effect will help you explain the mood and atmosphere in a piece of writing.

# Alliteration

Look at the following example of alliteration:

> It was a dull, desperately depressing day.

The 'd' sound makes the sentence feel heavy and slows it down, making the dull day seem even more depressing.

## ACTIVITY 2

**1** What mood or atmosphere is created in these examples?
- The sun shone, smiling down on the excited travellers.
- The violent violet lights flashed rapidly.
- The slithering snake slipped past.

Read the following passage, about an expert cake maker.

> She focused intently — fiercely even — on her way to
> piping the precise amount of filling into each and
> every one of the one hundred and fifty-six cupcakes
> that lined the racks on the stainless steel worktable
> in front of her — which was totally unnecessary. The
> fierce focusing, not the filling. She could fill a
> table of cupcakes blindfolded. In her sleep. With one
> hand tied behind her back. Possibly on one foot.
> She's never done it but she'd take the bet.
>
> Donna Kauffman, *Sugar Rush* (2011)

Alliteration of 'p' sound

Alliteration of 's' sound

Alliteration of 'f' sound

**2 a)** Think about how the narrator describes what the character is doing by using alliteration. For example, she says 'piping the precise amount of filling …' She is working carefully to make the perfect cakes. How does the alliteration make this seem an exact, precise act?

**b)** Write a short explanation of how this passage uses alliteration to create an effect on the reader.

This is the start of a Grade 5 response.

It is better to write about a few examples in detail than to try to write about lots of different ones very briefly.

The writer has created a precise, careful character in this passage by using a number of examples of alliteration. The first example is 'piping the precise amount of filling ...' where the 'p' sound creates a short, rapid feeling making the action seem quick and precise. It is like she has done this many times before.

This is Grade 5 standard because the student is able to pick out an example, support it with a quotation and then explain the effect on the reader, beginning to offer more than one interpretation.

Look back at your own response and improve it to this standard.

## 4 The effect of sentence structure

Writers' sentence structures are almost always varied. For instance, sentences can be deliberately constructed to be short and fragmented or long and flowing.

## Practising for success

### Using short sentences

Writers do not use short sentences just to make the text easier to understand; they use them to create specific effects.

### ACTIVITY 1

**1** Look at the following example of a series of short sentences and the student comment on it afterwards, and write an analysis of how these sentences are used.

> She paused. She was unsure. What should she do now? She paused again.

Reason given for short sentences

Effect explained

Here the writer uses short sentences to show the pauses, as you actually stop and start a lot, just like the character does. She does not know what to do next, so this is showing it is taking her a while to make her mind up.

Development of explanation

(Grade 4 standard)

A Grade 5 answer might add thoughts about the repetition of 'paused', or the total focus on one person 'She ... She ... She ...', or the way she is made to seem nervous because her thoughts come so hesitantly and without development.

Writers sometimes use short sentences following on from longer sentences, to create drama or emphasis. For example:

> They walked through the
> streets, past ruined houses,
> empty shops, through piles of
> rubbish and rubble from the
> bombardment. There was nothing
> left. Nothing at all.

The writer has used a longer sentence to describe a range of things the characters see. This is followed by two sentences decreasing in size. The first is a summary of what they see. The final sentence is even shorter, emphasising the total realisation that nothing is left, so it is a totally destroyed place.

(Grade 5)

Writers also use an **ellipsis** to create an incomplete sentence, leaving us to work out what might come next.

For example:

- He walked out and suddenly …
- They thought it was safe but now …
- She cried out, 'What are you doing? Where are you …?'

The first sentence doesn't end so there is a sense of suspense built up – we don't know yet what has happened to the character.

Write a short explanation for the effect of the other two sentences.

**2** Write your own comments on the effects here.

> Stop. Start. Stop. Start. The car moved slowly.
> Slowly. The traffic almost congealed …

It came suddenly. The pain hit her hard. She screamed in agony.

> The door was open and inside there seemed to be an endless array of delights: food of all kinds; drink in copious amounts and all the pleasures they could have dreamed of. Fantastic!

Write three examples of your own in which you use short sentences. For each one, explain why you have written them this way and what the effect is.

**Key term**

**Ellipsis**: three dots (…) which suggest there is more to come, leaving the reader to imagine what comes next.

Now, read the source below. It is an extract from *Bend it Like Beckham*, a novel about a young female football player. This is a moment where she is taking a crucial penalty.

> 'Come on, Jess!' That was Jules. 'You can do this.' I made a
> superhuman effort and ran towards the ball, but even as I hit it,
> I knew it wasn't right. I groaned as the ball hit the crossbar and
> ricocheted into the crowd. Now I knew exactly how Gareth Southgate,
> David Batty and all those other players who'd missed penalties for
> England felt. Like someone had grabbed hold of my insides and
> ripped them out. Gutted, in other words.
>
> Narinder Dhami, *Bend it Like Beckham* (2002)

**3** How does the writer use short sentences to create effect?

## Using longer sentences

An author might also choose to write longer sentences, also for dramatic effect.

Read the examples below.

> The lazy day stretched out for ever while they lay in the long grass dozing, thinking rich thoughts and gradually drifting off into sweet slumber under the warm, hazy sunshine, whilst neither had a care in the world and time was slowly, silently, stealthily passing by.

Now read the following student explanation on the above example.

Identifies use of long sentence

Brief comment on the effect of the long sentence

The writer uses a long sentence so it's a lazy day. The writer has used alliteration as well which also makes it seem as though time is passing slowly. There are also lots of commas used which list the qualities of what the sun is like and then they give the effect of time passing by 'slowly, silently, stealthily'.

(Grade 3 response)

Identification of another technique, but lacks examples

Identifies use of commas with example and brief explanation

### ACTIVITY 2

**1** Write an improvement of this response, making it a Grade 5 answer by explaining the effects more clearly.

Longer sentences can also be used to list things, to describe to the reader a busy place with lots going on, or an action-packed scene. For example:

> He looked around and all he could see was chaos. There were people everywhere, standing, sitting, lying about, some with long trousers, jackets or coats on, or just simply a t-shirt and shorts as if they had been dragged from their room in the middle of the night without a moment to decide what to put on and grabbed the nearest things available to them.

Discussion point

The atmosphere here is one of 'chaos'. With a friend, discuss the effect of the long second sentence. How is the reader expected to react? Explain.

# Repetition

## ACTIVITY 3

Repetition can also be used by writers within longer sentences to build an effect.

**1** What effect does the repetition of the word 'past' have in the passage below?

> The train began to pick up speed as it moved down hill, quickly rumbling past trees, past houses, past hedges and small people looking up from whatever they were doing as if interrupted from their tranquil existence by something from another world, loud and out of control and not a part of their lives at all.

Sometimes, a long sentence might build to a **climax**.

**2** Add to the sentence below, so that it finishes on a moment of high drama. Add several lines, if you wish.

**Key term**

**Climax:** a big finish.

> I was desperately hanging on to the ledge and the wind was blowing and my arms were tiring and I was praying that someone would come and rescue me, then ...

Read this exam Question 2, based on the passage below:

**How does the writer use language to describe the events in the extract below?**

> At first I could see nothing; the darkness had a texture so dense I fancied my outstretched hands were pushing against giant elastic cobwebs. The ground under me conspired to **disorientate** me. It was spongy and silent under my uncertain feet, no crackling branches or noisy heather to reassure me that I walked on the earth and owned it; I felt this forest now owned me. After slapping head-first into a few low branches I became accustomed to the gloom and began to pick my way more confidently through the trees, fixing my gaze on the back of Anita's shoes which seemed to glow like **low, uneven landing lights**. Then I suddenly realised that I could not hear the fairground any more. It had been replaced by a much louder noise, a low breathing made up of night breeze, whispering leaves, insects humming in morse code and the sporadic mournful hoots of a lone high owl.
>
> Meera Syal, *Anita and Me* (2002)

**disorientate** means to be confused about where they are

**low, uneven landing lights** are used on aircraft to light up the runway they are landing on

To respond effectively, you would need to be aware of the different uses of language you have studied in this unit.

**1** Read the response below and discuss the strengths and weaknesses of **Response A**, a Grade 1 response, and how it could be improved to earn a higher grade.

## Response A

The person could not see anything and it was dark. It sounds like the ground is spongy and it was a forest. It was quiet as no branches cracked but she banged her head on branches. It was quiet as she couldn't hear any fairground sounds. She could hear whispering leaves and a breeze. There is onomatopoeia here.

**2** Now read this extract from a second response – **Response B** – and study the annotations to see why it would receive a Grade 5.

## Response B

Identification of alliteration

Comment is given about the effect of the alliteration

Onomatopoeia is identified

The narrator uses lots of language techniques to create an atmosphere in the passage. There is alliteration used on 'spongy and silent' and to make it sound quiet the 's' sound is repeated, like a shhh sound. When she uses onomatopoeia with 'whispering leaves' you can hear the rustling sound of the leaves in the word 'whispering' like the leaves are talking to her. It's quite scary really.

Comment is given on the effect of the onomatopoeia, with some extended interpretation

**3** Continue **Response B**, trying to use the **PEA** technique – giving more than one explanation – when you can.

Assessment comment

Response B would earn a Grade 5 mark, because it answers the question, picking out several language techniques, selecting some relevant quotations and explaining them. The student uses some appropriate subject terminology such as onomatopoeia and alliteration.

## Test yourself

Read the passage below, and answer the exam-style question that follows. The passage is from a novel written from the point of view of a young boy, Christopher, who has Asperger's Syndrome. As a result of this he is very clever but he has problems interacting with people.

On the bus on the way to school next morning we passed 4 red cars in a row which meant that it was a Good Day, so I decided not to be sad.

Mr Jeavons, the psychologist at the school, once asked me why 4 red cars in a row made it a Good Day, and 3 red cars in a row made it a Quite Good Day, and 5 red cars in a row made it a Super Good Day, and why 4 yellow cars in a row made it a Black Day, which is a day when I don't speak to anyone and sit on my own reading books and don't eat my lunch and Take No Risks. He said that I was clearly a very logical person, so he was surprised that I should think like this because it wasn't very logical.

I said that I liked things to be in a nice order. And one way of things being in a nice order was to be logical. Especially if those things were numbers or an argument. But there were other ways of putting things in a nice order. And that was why I had Good Days and Black Days. And I said that some people who worked in an office came out of their house in the morning and saw that the sun was shining and it made them feel happy, or the way that it was raining and it made them feel sad, but the only difference was the weather and if they worked in an office the weather didn't have anything to do with whether they had a good day or a bad day.

I said that when Father got up in the morning he always put his trousers on before he put his socks on and it wasn't logical but he always did it that way, because he liked things in a nice order, too. Also whenever he went upstairs he went up two at a time always starting with his right foot.

Mr Jeavons said that I was a very clever boy.

Mark Haddon, *The Curious Incident of the Dog in the Night-Time* (2004)

**How does Haddon use language to create effects in this extract?**

(8 marks)

*What you have learned*

**In this unit you have learned to identify and write about:**
- language techniques that writers use in literature
- how to explain the effect of the techniques used.

**In this unit you will learn about:**
⇨ the kinds of structural devices used by writers
⇨ why writers use **structural devices**.

## What this unit involves

This unit deals with Paper 1, Question 3.

You will have to answer a question on the fiction text focusing on structural devices the writer has used, what effect they have and the impression they create.

This question is worth 8 marks, which means you will have 8 or 9 minutes to answer it.

## Key Term

**Structural devices:** how the writing is organised, its main features and its focus.

## 1 How writers use openings

Writers need the opening of their text to be interesting. They sometimes use:

- a variety of sentence lengths
- varied paragraphing
- a close focus on a specific theme or idea
- a focus on a specific character or group of characters, setting or contrast.

# Practising for success

### ACTIVITY 1

Read this opening.

When summer comes to the North Woods, time slows down. And some days it stops altogether. The sky, gray and **lowering** for much of the year, becomes an ocean of blue, so vast and brilliant you can't help but stop what you're doing – pinning wet sheets to the line maybe, or **shucking** a bushel of corn on the back steps – to stare up at it. Locusts whir in the bushes, coaxing you out of the sun and under the boughs, and the heat stills the air, heavy and sweet with the scent of **balsam**.

Jennifer Donnelly, *A Gathering Light* (2004)

**lowering** means frowning

**shucking** is removing shells from corn

**balsam** is a substance from trees used for fragrance

1 Explain what the opening two sentences make the reader feel. How does the writer make us feel that way?

Writers use opening sentences to immediately grab the attention of the reader and give us an impression of a situation/character/event. Always look carefully at the opening of the text in an examination and try to explain what impact it has on the reader.

2 The passage then moves on to develop the description of the scene. With a friend, discuss the heavy details included, the sentence lengths, and how a sense of stillness is created.

This is a very different opening:

> I stepped out of the car and into the hot thick heat of August in Georgia.
>
> 'Awesome,' I murmured, sliding my sunglasses on top of my head. Thanks to the humidity, my hair felt like it had tripled in size. I could feel it trying to devour my sunglasses like some sort of **carnivorous** jungle plant. 'I always wondered what it would be like to live in somebody's mouth.'
>
> Rachel Hawkins, *Hex Hall* (2010)

**carnivorous** plants are those that eat animals

3 Why is the first sentence effective here?

4 How does the writer make the scene feel uncomfortable for the narrator? Think about how the writer uses words such as 'hot thick heat', 'devour' and 'carnivorous jungle plant'.

5 What impression do we get of the person speaking? Why?

6 What might this story be about? Give your reasons.

7 How does the writer create humour here? What impact does the humour have on the reader?

Now read this opening from a zombie horror novel, set in a world where everyone over the age of fourteen has been struck down by a deadly virus, making them go mad.

Small Sam was playing in the car park behind Waitrose when the grown-ups took him. He'd been with some of the little kids having a battle with an odd assortment of action figures, when it happened. They weren't supposed to play outside without a guard, but it was a lovely sunny day and the little kids got bored indoors. Sam wasn't the youngest of the group, but he was the smallest. That's why they called him Small Sam. There had originally been two other Sams, Big Sam and Curly Sam, who had curly hair. Big Sam had been killed a few months ago, but Small Sam was stuck with the name.

It was probably because of his size that the grown-ups went for him. They were like that — they picked out the youngsters, the weaklings, the little ones. In the panic of the attack the rest of Sam's gang got back safely inside, but Sam was cut off and the roving pack of grown-ups trapped him in a corner.

They had come over a side wall led by a big mother in a track-suit that might once have been pink but was now so filthy and greasy it looked like grey plastic. She had a fat, egg-like body on top of long, skinny legs. Her back was bent and she ran stooped over, but surprisingly fast, her arms held wide like a scorpion's claws, her dirty blonde hair hanging straight down. Her face blank and stupid. Breathing through her mouth.

Charles Higson, *The Enemy* (2010)

Now read this Grade 5 student analysis of the extract.

Introduction to a key character is picked out

Discusses what the purpose of the opening is

This is an effective opening as the writer immediately introduces us to a key character, Small Sam, and we are straight into a key event where he is taken by the adults. The fact that this is a dramatic and an unusual event makes this an interesting opening making us ask questions such as: why would adults take a small child, why are they so threatening and what will happen to the boy, so a lot of suspense is created.

Point about the build-up of information

There is a gradual build up to the incident. The first paragraph introduces Sam Small and tells us a bit about his character such as why he is called Small Sam and his age as 'the youngest of the group'. This makes him seem weaker and an easy target for the adults.

Explanation of effect of quotation

In contrast, the second paragraph gives us information on what the adults generally do and how they pick on 'the weaklings'. The adults are made to seem threatening as a 'pack' which makes them seem like wolves hunting. Again, we are intrigued to know why they are acting like this.

More comment, support, and explanation of the structure ('In contrast')

The third paragraph begins to describe the event in more detail, with some lively description of the characters, such as the 'big mother'. We are given almost a comic or horrible description of this woman, as 'fat, egg-like body' is a comic image to behold and she has 'scorpion's claws' which again is threatening and we want to know why she is behaving and looking like this.

Discusses the overall effect of the opening on the reader

Embedded quotation

**8** Make your own comments on what is good about the last paragraph of this response.

**9** What effective techniques can you see in the opening below?

Sunlight dances over the little girl's dark curls as she toddles clumsily through the dry grass. Her rosy cheeks dimple as she grins, her green eyes sparkling as she lunges sticky fingers towards the camera. Suddenly she trips.

The picture immediately jolts and twists into the grass, continuing at a skewed angle as a chestnut-haired woman rushes over to the child. But she is not crying. The screen fills with silent giggles as her mother scoops her up, her beautiful face filled with tenderness as she cuddles her daughter tightly, protectively, holding her so close it seems she'll never let go… The picture begins to blur…

I click the remote and the image flicks off, plunging the room into darkness. I stare at the blank screen. It's weird to watch your memories on screen, like watching a movie. It's like somewhere, in some wonderful world, those moments are trapped, bottled, to be enjoyed again. I wonder if Heaven's like that – that you get to choose the best moments of your life and just relive them over and over. I hope so.

Katie Dale, *Someone Else's Life* (2012)

Copy the table below and write a list of techniques. Find a supporting quotation from the source to illustrate it, explaining the effect of this on the reader.

| TECHNIQUE | SUPPORTING EVIDENCE AND EXPLANATION OF EFFECT |
|---|---|
| Setting a clear scene | 'Sunlight dances over the little girl's dark curls'<br><br>Here the writer makes the atmosphere seem happy and relaxed as we have sunlight dancing (personification) so it feels like an upbeat moment. |
|  |  |
|  |  |
|  |  |
|  |  |

## 2 How writers use endings

Effective endings leave the reader wanting more or feeling satisfied that what they have read has ended satisfactorily.

## Practising for success

Read the ending of *Spies*. The narrator takes a moment to calmly reflect on things – the story has rapidly moved from place to place.

> Now all the mysteries have been resolved, or as resolved as they're ever likely to be. All that remains is the familiar slight ache in the bones, like an old wound when the weather changes. **Heimweh or Fernweh**? A longing to be there or a longing to be here, even though I'm here already. Or to be both at once? Or to be neither, but in the old country of the past, that will never be reached again in either place?
>
> Time to go. So, once again — thank you everyone. Thank you for having me.
>
> And, on the air as I turn the corner at the end of the street, a sudden faint breath of something familiar. Even here, after all. Even here.
>
> Michael Frayn, *Spies* (2002)

**Heimweh or Fernweh** is German for homesickness or wanting to get away

## ACTIVITY 1

An ending can deliberately be structured to make the reader think or feel a certain emotion.

1 The writer begins this end section by using slightly longer sentences. What does this show the reader about his thought process?

2 Why has the writer chosen to directly speak to the reader? *'So, once again…'*

3 What impact does using short sentences such as *'Time to go.'* have on the reader?

4 What are we supposed to think when we read the final paragraph? Is he happy or sad? How do we know?

Read the following source taken from the ending of the first in a series of novels where everyone over the age of 15 vanishes.

The pleading speech shows the horrific nature of his death

'Help me,' EZ whispered. 'Sam...'

EZ's eyes were on Sam. Pleading. Fading. Then just staring, blank.

The only sounds now came from the worms. Their hundreds of mouths seemed to make a single sound, one big mouth chewing wetly.

An unpleasant description of the horrible event

A worm spilled from EZ's mouth.

Sam raised his hands, palms out.

The reaction of Albert as be watches

'Sam, no!' Albert yelled. Then in a quieter voice, 'He's already dead.'

'Albert's right, man. Don't burn them, they're staying in the field, don't give them a reason to come after us,' Edilio hissed.

The black worms swarmed over and through EZ's body. Like ants swarmed over and through EZ's body. Like ants swarming a dead beetle.

The final line of the novel is shocking

It felt like a very long time before the worms slithered away and tunnelled back into the earth.

What they left behind was no longer recognisable as a human being.

Michael Grant, *Gone* (2009)

**5** Look at the ending of the first line and the use of the ellipsis (...). What is the effect of the ellipsis here? ('Sam...')

**6** Look at the use of short sentences in paragraph 2. 'EZ's eyes were on Sam. Pleading. Fading. Then just staring, blank.' There are four short sentences in this brief paragraph, used to show the desperation of EZ's final moments.

The words used are emotive. What do they make you feel?

**7** What is the impact of the speech on the reader in the sixth paragraph: '"Sam, no!" Albert yelled. Then in a quieter voice, "He's already dead."'?

**8** What does the writer expect us to think by using the repetition of 'like ants' in the paragraph: 'The black worms swarmed over and through EZ's body. Like ants swarmed over and through EZ's body. Like ants swarming a dead beetle.'?

**9** Why do you think the writer ended the novel with 'What they left behind was no longer recognisable as a human being.'? Why is it an effective ending to this extract you have read?

**10** Using the information you have gathered from answering the questions above, answer the question:
**How has the writer structured the text to end the novel effectively?**

## 3 Using conversation and narrative

Writers often use conversation and narrative to develop their ideas.

For example, a writer may begin by telling us about their thoughts and feelings or offering some general background before focusing on something more specific. Of course, the opening may leave a number of questions unanswered, which creates intrigue for the reader.

# Practising for success

Read the extract below.

It happened every year, was almost a ritual. And this was his eighty-second birthday. When, as usual, the flower was delivered, he took off the wrapping paper and then picked up the telephone to call Detective Superintendent Morell who, when he retired, had moved to Lake Siljan in Dalarna. They were not only the same age, they had been born on the same day – which was something of an irony under the circumstances. The old policeman was sitting with his coffee, waiting, expecting the call.

"It arrived."

"What is it this year?"

"I don't know what kind it is. I'll have to get someone to tell me what it is. It's white."

"No letter, I suppose."

"Just the flower. The frame is the same kind as last year. One of those do-it-yourself ones."

"Postmark?"

"Stockholm."

"Handwriting?"

"Same as always, all in capitals. Upright, neat lettering."

With that, the subject was exhausted, and not another word was exchanged for almost a minute. The retired policeman leaned back in his kitchen chair and drew on his pipe. He knew he was no longer expected to come up with a pithy comment or any sharp question which would shed a new light on the case. Those days had long since passed, and the exchange between the two men seemed like a ritual attaching to a mystery which no-one else in the whole world had the least interest in unravelling.

Stieg Larsson, *The Girl With The Dragon Tattoo* (2011)

## ACTIVITY 1

1 To begin with, the narrative is quite general. What are we told about in the opening paragraph?

2 What do we learn from the conversation? Copy and fill in the table below.

| WHAT WE LEARN | SUPPORTING EVIDENCE FROM THE SOURCE |
|---|---|
| something has arrived | 'It arrived.' |
| | |
| | |

3 What does the conversation add to what has gone before? Does it make the story more or less interesting?

4 The conversation is sandwiched between the two other paragraphs. How does the final paragraph develop what has gone before?

5 Read right through the extract again. How does the writer use the structure to interest the reader?

Read the following opening to a Grade 4 student response to question 5 above.

What is good about the way it examines the author's use of structure? How could you improve it to earn a higher grade?

The writer begins by setting the scene. We are told that 'It happened every year.' We don't know what 'it' is yet, but beginning this way means we have to read on to find out what it is. The suspense is built up in the way this is all described with a list of actions 'took off the wrapping paper ... call Detective Superintendent Morell.' This all builds mystery for the reader.

We then move into a section of conversation with several brief sentences giving us a sense of the characters and a gradual increase of information as to what the mystery item is. We learn in small stages that it is 'white', that there is no letter and that it is a flower in a frame. It has come from Stockholm. This gradual increase of information helps the reader to get a clearer picture of what is being described with a sense of mystery sustained.

6 Complete the answer by writing about the final paragraph of the extract.

I still remember the day my father took me to the Cemetery of Forgotten Books for the first time. It was the early summer of 1945, and we walked through the streets of a Barcelona trapped beneath ashen skies as dawn poured over Rambla de Santa Monica in a wreath of liquid copper. 'Daniel, you mustn't tell anyone what you're about to see today,' my father warned. 'Not even your friend Tomas. No one.'

'Not even Mummy?'

My father sighed, hiding behind the sad smile that followed him like a shadow all through his life. 'Of course you can tell her,' he answered, heavy-hearted. 'We keep no secrets from her. You can tell her everything.'

Shortly after the Civil War, an outbreak of cholera had taken my mother away. We buried her in Montjuïc on my fourth birthday. The only thing I can recall is that it rained all day and all night, and that when I asked my father whether heaven was crying, he couldn't bring himself to reply. Six years later my mother's absence remained in the air around us, a deafening silence that I had not yet learned to stifle with words. My father and I lived in a modest apartment on Calle Santa Ana, a stone's throw from the church square. The apartment was directly above the bookshop, a legacy from my grandfather, that specialized in rare collectors' editions and secondhand books – an enchanted bazaar, which my father hoped would one day be mine. I was raised among books, making invisible friends in pages that seemed cast from dust and whose smell I carry on my hands to this day. As a child I learned to fall asleep talking to my mother in the darkness of my bedroom, telling her about the day's events, my adventures at school, and the things I had been taught. I couldn't hear her voice or feel her touch, but her radiance and her warmth haunted every corner of our home, and I believed, with the innocence of those who can still count their age on their ten fingers, that if I closed my eyes and spoke to her, she would be able to hear me wherever she was. Sometimes my father would listen to me from the dining room, crying in silence.

On that June morning, I woke up screaming at first light.

My heart was pounding in my chest as if my very soul was trying to escape. My father hurried into my room and held me in his arms, trying to calm me.

Carlos Ruiz Zafón, *The Shadow of the Wind* (2005)

39

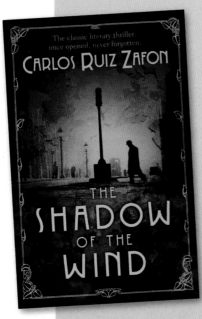

1  In a group, answer the following questions:

a) Most of the narration is the boy reflecting on the death of his mother and commenting on his father. Why has the writer given us so much detail from the boy himself?

b) Why is the use of speech so effective?

c) Look at the list: '*As a child I learned to fall asleep talking to my mother in the darkness of my bedroom, telling her about the day's events, my adventures at school, and the things I had been taught.*' What does this list show us about their relationship?

d) What is the effect of the one-sentence paragraph: '*On that June morning, I woke up screaming at first light.*'? Why is it more effective as it has come from the narrative point of view of the boy?

2  Write a full answer to this question:

**What is the effect of the narrative structure of this passage?**

In your response, you can use all the information from answering the questions above.

Remember that the material you are writing about has been written by someone and that you must write about how the writer creates the text, not as if the people and events being described are real.

Try not to just retell the story, but make sure you are answering the question and explaining why the writer tells the story as they have: it is always to have a specific effect on the reader.

## Test yourself

Read the source on page 41, then answer this question:

*How has the writer used structure to gain the reader's interest?*

You could write about:

- what the writer focuses your attention on at the beginning
- how and why the writer changes this focus as the extract develops
- any other structural features that interest you.

In this story, the narrator, Zoe, has a secret. She tells her story through a series of letters to Stuart Harris, an inmate on Death Row, waiting to be executed.

Dear Mr S Harris,

Ignore the blob of red in the top left corner. It's jam not blood, though I don't think I need to tell you the difference. It wasn't your wife's jam the police found on your shoe.

The jam in the corner's from my sandwich. Homemade raspberry. Gran made it. She's been dead seven years and making that jam was the last thing she did. Sort of. If you ignore the weeks she spent in hospital attached to one of those heart things that goes beep beep if you're lucky or beeeeeeeeeeeeeeeeeeeeeeeeep if you're not. That was the sound echoing round the hospital room seven years ago. Beeeeeeeeeeeeeeeeeeeeeeep. My little sister was born six months later and Dad named her after Gran. Dorothy Constance. When Dad stopped grieving, he decided to shorten it. My sister is small and round so we ended up calling her Dot.

My other sister, Soph, is ten. They've both got long blonde hair and green eyes and pointy noses, but Soph is tall and thin and darker skinned, like Dot's been rolled out and crisped in the oven for ten minutes. I'm different. Brown hair. Brown eyes. Medium height. Medium weight. Ordinary, I suppose. To look at me, you'd never guess my secret.

I struggled to eat the sandwich in the end. The jam wasn't off or anything because it lasts for years in sterilised jars.

At least that's what Dad says when Mum turns up her nose. It's pointy too. Her hair's the same colour as my sisters' but shorter and a bit wavy. Dad's is more like mine except with grey bits above his ears, and he's got this thing called heterochromia, which means one eye's brown but the other's lighter. Blue if it's bright outside, grey if it's overcast. The sky in a socket, I once said, and Dad got these dimples right in the middle of his cheeks, and I don't know if any of this really matters but I suppose it's good to give you a picture of my family before I tell you what I came in here to say.

via air mail

Annabel Pitcher, *Ketchup Clouds* (2012)

## What you have learned

In this unit you have learned to analyse and write about:
- how writers use different techniques to structure their writing
- the importance of how writers structure openings
- the effect of endings
- how writers use narrators.

In this unit you will learn how to analyse and write about:

⇨ what characters look like and how they behave
⇨ how writers use viewpoint
⇨ how writers reveal relationships
⇨ how the themes of the story are explored
⇨ how writers use settings
⇨ how to evaluate what the writer has produced.

## What this unit involves

This unit deals with Paper 1, Question 4. You will have to:

- write about a fiction text
- write about the techniques the writer has used
- say how successful he has been
- support your ideas with quotations.

The question could relate to character, relationships, themes or settings. It is an important question which carries 20 marks. You will have just over 20 minutes to write your answer.

## 1 How characters are described

Writers describe characters so that the reader can imagine them more easily. This usually happens when they are first introduced, or soon after. A writer may start by describing:

- what they look like
- how they move
- how they speak
- the way they behave.

They may provide considerable detail, or they may leave much to the reader's imagination.

## Practising for success

Look at this description of Ralph, one of a group of boys who have just crash landed on a deserted island.

He was old enough, twelve years and a few months, to have lost the prominent tummy of childhood and not yet old enough for adolescence to have made him awkward. You could see now that he might make a boxer, as far as width and heaviness of shoulders went, but there was a mildness about his mouth and eyes that proclaimed no devil. He patted the palm trunk softly, and, forced at last to believe in the reality of the island, laughed delightedly again and stood on his head. He turned neatly on to his feet, jumped down to the beach, knelt and swept a double armful of sand into a pile against his chest. Then he sat back and looked at the water with bright, excited eyes.

William Golding, *Lord of the Flies* (1954)

## ACTIVITY 1

**1** Copy the table below and write down the things you learn about Ralph in this extract. Find at least six things.

| DESCRIPTION | WHAT THIS TELLS YOU ABOUT HIM |
|---|---|
| 'lost the prominent tummy of childhood' | He is not a child any more but becoming older – he is nearly in his teens. |
| | |
| | |

See how this Grade 5 student wrote about Ralph based on this extract:

Use of quotation to illustrate point

A development of the idea with another characteristic and another quotation from the source

Golding presents Ralph as a boy who is growing up. He has 'lost the prominent tummy of childhood' showing that he is not a chubby baby anymore, but he is not quite old enough to be awkward like a teenager can be. He describes his physical appearance saying he could make a 'boxer' as he has broad shoulders, so he is strong-looking. Whilst he is strong he has a gentleness about him 'that proclaimed no devil' so he is friendly and pleasant, even if he is strong looking as well. He seems almost the perfect boy.

Two comments on the description of Ralph

Another quotation and a different characteristic of Ralph is identified

Moving into PEA, offering extended interpretations

A summary of all the description, making a judgement and evaluating the source

**2** Write about what we learn about Ralph in the final five lines of the extract, matching the qualities of the Grade 5 response.

How does the language help us build a clearer picture of what Ralph is like?

**3** Read the following question and the notes that follow on page 44:

**Evaluate** the way Ralph is described in the last five lines of the extract from 'He patted the palm trunk softly…' to the end of the passage.

> ### Examiner comment
>
> Notice how the student uses quotations by just picking short phrases and words rather than long sections from the source. It is better to use quotations like this rather than simply copying long sections, which will not gain you any extra marks.

> ### Key term
>
> **Evaluation**: this means to determine the importance, the value or worth of what the writer has done in a piece of writing.

An answer to this question might be:

> The writer chooses to show us the childish side of Ralph to remind us that he is just a boy, after all, and although he is thoughtful, he likes to run around and play, like most young boys do. This is an important reminder to the reader that they are all children.
>
> (Grade 5)

The highlighted part of the answer is where the student is evaluating the importance of what is described here. The student has given a number of reasons why the writer has shown the childish side of Ralph and has concluded by linking this with the importance of the effect on the reader.

Boost your grade

Write an answer to the following question:

Evaluate Golding's description of Ralph in the first five lines of the passage.

Begin: 'Golding gives us a clear description of Ralph and what he is like ...'

## 2 How character is revealed in a first-person narrative

A first-person narrative has a narrator speaking directly to the reader.

### Advantages and disadvantages of first-person narrative

An advantage of this is that the reader will get to know the character better and feel they know their thoughts and feelings.

A disadvantage is that what we are told by the character may not be totally true as it comes from their point of view and, therefore, can be affected by their views and understanding.

## Practising for success

The following passage is written from the viewpoint of a 10-year-old boy, Jamie, whose sister has died in the terrorist bombings in London in July 2005.

My sister Rose lives on the mantelpiece. Well, some of her does. Three of her fingers, her right elbow and her kneecap are buried in a graveyard in London. Mum and Dad had a big argument when the police found ten bits of her body. Mum wanted a grave that she could visit. Dad wanted a cremation and to sprinkle the ashes in the sea. That's what Jasmine told me anyway. She remembers more than I do. I was only five when it happened. Jasmine was ten. She was Rose's twin. Still is, according to Mum and Dad. They dressed Jas the same for years after the funeral — flowery dresses, cardigans, those flat shoes with buckles that Rose used to love. I reckon that's why Mum ran off with the man from the support group seventy one days ago. When Jas cut off all her hair, dyed it pink and got her nose pierced on her fifteenth birthday, she didn't look like Rose anymore and my parents couldn't hack it.

They each got five bits. Mum put hers in a fancy white coffin beneath a fancy white headstone that says *My Angel* on it. Dad burned a collarbone, two ribs, a bit of skull and a little toe and put the ashes in a golden urn. So they both got their own way, but surprise surprise it didn't make them happy. Mum says the graveyard's too depressing to visit. And every anniversary Dad tries to spread the ashes but changes his mind at the last minute. Something seems to happen right when Rose is about to be tipped into the sea. One year in Devon there were loads of these swarming silver fish that looked like they couldn't wait to eat my sister. And another year in Cornwall a seagull poohed on the urn just as Dad was about to open it. I just started to laugh but Jas looked so sad I stopped.

Annabel Pitcher, *My Sister Lives on the Mantlepiece* (2011)

## ACTIVITY 1

**Discussion point**

1 With a friend, discuss the following questions:
- Jamie, as the narrator, tells us a lot about what has happened in the past. How accurate is this likely to be compared to what was actually happened?
- What could have caused Jamie to get anything wrong or to change anything?
- Which details do you think are most likely to be wrong or less accurate?

2 Using the ideas you have collected, write a response to the question:

**What impression do you get of Jamie in this extract?**

Now read this extract from a little further into the same chapter:

We moved out of London to get away from it all. Dad knew someone who knew someone who rung him up about a job on a building site in the Lake District. He hadn't worked in London for ages. There's a recession, which means the country has no money, so hardly anything's getting built. When we got the job in Ambleside, we sold our flat and rented a cottage and left Mum in London. I bet Jas five whole pounds that Mum would come to wave us off. She didn't make me pay when I lost. In the car Jas said *Let's play I Spy*, but she couldn't guess *Something beginning with R*, even though Roger was sitting right on my lap, purring as if he was giving her a clue.

It's so different here. There are massive mountains that are tall enough to poke God up the bum, hundreds of trees, and it's quiet. *No people*, I said as we found the cottage down a twisty lane and I looked out of the window for somebody to play with.

Our cottage is the complete opposite of our flat in Finsbury Park. It's white, not brown, big not small, old not new. Art's my favourite subject at school and, if I painted the buildings as people, I would turn the cottage into a crazy old granny, smiling with no teeth. The flat would be a serious soldier all smart and squashed up in a row of identical men. Mum would love that. She's a teacher at an art college and I reckon she'd show every single one of her students if I sent her my pictures.

Even though Mum's in London I was happy to leave the flat behind. My room was tiny but I wasn't allowed to swap with Rose 'cos she's dead and her stuff's sacred. That was the answer I always got whenever I asked if I could move. Rose's room is sacred, James. Don't go in there, James, it's sacred. I don't see what's sacred about a bunch of old dolls, a smelly pink duvet and a bald teddy. Didn't feel that sacred when I jumped up and down on Rose's bed one day when I got home from school. Jas made me stop but she promised not to tell.

Annabel Pitcher, *My Sister Lives on the Mantlepiece*, 2011

**3** What words and phrases tell you that Jamie was not as happy in his old home?

Make a list of them.

**4** Why is Jamie unhappy with his parents?

**5** What does Jamie tell us about his old life, his new home, his family and his feelings? Support your ideas with details from the source.

Look at sentences like:

- *'There are massive mountains that are tall enough to poke God up the bum, hundreds of trees, and it's quiet.'*

- *'The flat would be a serious soldier all smart and squashed up in a row of identical men. Mum would love that.'*

- *'Didn't feel that sacred when I jumped up and down on Rose's bed one day when I got home from school one day.'*

 Evaluate the way the writer has presented Jamie –
what do we think about him by the end?

Hint: Think about the sentence lengths, how details are listed and the effect of details.

# 3 Presenting relationships

Writers often use their narrative to present relationships between
characters. This can be achieved using first- or third-person narration
or a combination of the two.

### Third-person narrative

A third-person narrative is a story written from the viewpoint of
someone watching the whole scene occur, but not actually involved in
the action themselves, using 'he', 'she' and 'they'. They are **omniscient**
and know everything that is happening.

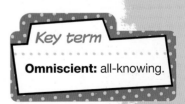

**Key term**

**Omniscient:** all-knowing.

## Practising for success

Read this extract, which shows two boys, Hooper and Kingshaw, lost in the woods at night and having to sleep outside. Hooper has injured himself and Kingshaw is looking after him.

Hooper was asleep. He lay with his legs all pulled up and his thumb in his mouth. Because of the bang on his head, Kingshaw had given him the anorak, to roll up for a pillow.

He felt protective towards Hooper, and patient with him, now, since finding him in the stream. He had become more important, somehow, because he had been so near to dying. He might easily have died, if the water had come up over his face, or if he had bashed his head much harder. Perhaps he might still die. People caught pneumonia from having been in the water. Or something might have happened inside his head, from the bump. There was no way of telling.

Susan Hill, *I'm the King of the Castle* (1970)

### ACTIVITY 1

Read this exam question:

**Write a short paragraph evaluating how the author reveals Kingshaw's feelings about Hooper. Use evidence from the passage to support your comments.**

This is a Grade 2 standard response:

A general comment on what is happening

Identifies structural technique and a brief, undeveloped comment on its effect

The narrator writes about Kingshaw looking at Hooper while he is asleep. He feels protective towards him because he had been close to dying. He imagines Hooper dying and how easily it may have happened. There are a few short sentences which show he is thinking. It seems he is worried he may still die.

Identifies Kingshaw's feelings but without going into detail

Comment on how he feels but lacks detail

This answer does not use any quotations from the passage.

**1** Write your own more detailed answer to the question, aiming for Grade 5.

# First-person narrative

Many relationships are presented from the viewpoint of one character as in the passage below. We get an individual's view of a relationship.

When we were children, Hassan and I used to climb the poplar trees in the driveway of my father's house and annoy the neighbours by reflecting sunlight into their homes with a **shard** of mirror. We would sit across from each other on a pair of high branches, our naked feet dangling, our trouser pockets filled with dried mulberries and walnuts. We took turns with the mirror as we ate the mulberries, pelted each other with them, giggling, laughing. I can still see Hassan up on that tree, sunlight flickering through the leaves on his almost perfectly round face, a face like a Chinese doll chiseled from hardwood: his flat, broad nose and slanting, narrow eyes like bamboo leaves, eyes that looked, depending on the light, gold, green, even sapphire. I can still see his tiny low-set ears and that pointed stub of a chin, a meaty appendage that looked like it was added as a mere afterthought. And the **cleft lip**, just left of mid-line, where the Chinese doll maker's instrument may have slipped, or perhaps he had simply grown tired and careless.

Sometimes, up in those trees, I talked Hassan into firing walnuts with his slingshot at the neighbor's one-eyed German shepherd. Hassan never wanted to, but if I asked, *really* asked, he wouldn't deny me. Hassan never denied me anything. And he was deadly with his slingshot.

And he never told on me. Never told anybody that the mirror, like shooting walnuts at the neighbor's dog, was always my idea.

Khaled Housseini, *The Kite Runner* (2003)

**shard** is a broken piece

**cleft lip** is a split in the upper lip which occurred before birth

## ACTIVITY 1

1 What age do you think Hassan is, judging by the details given?
2 What does the narrator tell you about Hassan? Write a list of information.
3 How does Hassan react to the narrator?
4 What does the narrator think about Hassan?
5 Evaluate how successfully the writer presents the relationship between the boys in the passage. Your evaluation could include comment on:
   - how well we understand their relationship
   - memorable details
   - the overall effect on the reader.

## 4 How writers present themes

A theme is a key idea or topic that an author explores through a story and the interaction of its characters. Some examples of possible themes are:

- power/authority
- love and hate
- family relationships
- war
- growing up.

## Practising for success

Ben Elton's novel *The First Casualty* creates the horrors of World War I in vivid detail.

The extract below describes an incident in the trenches, a long, narrow channel dug out in the ground to protect the men. The conditions were poor and no one knew when they would be called on to face almost certain death.

'You there,' cried a voice, trying to make itself heard above the roar of artillery that thundered up from the guns at the rear. 'Military Police! Make way. I must get past. I simply must get past.'

Perhaps the man heard, perhaps he didn't. But if he did, he did not make way, but continued to plod steadily towards his goal. The officer could do no more than travel in his wake, cursing this ponderous beast of burden and hoping to find a point where the duckboard grew wide enough to let him pass safely. It was doubly frustrating for him to be so obstructed, for he knew enough about the nature of an attack to see that this fellow would not be advancing in the first wave. His job would be to follow on, using his wire and tools to help consolidate the gains made by the boys with the bayonets. The impatient officer did not expect any gains to be made. No gains of any significance anyway.

There had not been any in the battle before this one, nor had there been in the one preceding that. Still, even gains of a few yards would need consolidation, new trenches to be dug and fresh wire laid. And so the **pack mule** plodded on.

Then the mule slipped. His heavily nailed boot skidded on the wet **duckboard** and with scarcely a cry he fell sideways into the mud and was gone, sucked instantly beneath the surface.

'Man in the mud!' the officer shouted, although he knew it was already too late. 'Bring a rope! A rope, I say, for God's sake!'

**pack mule** is someone carrying a load on his back

**duckboards** are boards laid out to form a path over muddy ground

> But there was no rope to hand. Even if there had been one, and time to slip it around the sinking man, it is doubtful whether four of his comrades pulling together would have had the strength to draw him forth from the swamp that sucked at him. And there was no room on the duckboard for four men to stand together, or even two, and so slippery were the wire-bound planks that any rescue attempt would have resulted in the rescuers sharing the same fate as the man they hoped to save.
>
> And so the man drowned in mud.
>
> Dead and buried in a single moment.

Ben Elton, *The First Casualty* (2005)

## ACTIVITY 1

1 What is the writer saying about war?

2 How does the writer make the drama and horror clear to the reader?

Copy the table below and add extra details of your own.

| QUOTATION | EXPLANATION |
|---|---|
| 'Military Police! Make way. I must get past. I simply must get past.' | |
| 'Bring a rope! A rope, I say, for God's sake!' | The short sentences and use of exclamation marks show the desperation of the man to get a rope quickly so that they can rescue the man in the mud. |
| Dead and buried in a single moment. | |

Read the following Grade 5 answer to this question:

**By creating a sense of desperation and despair, how successful is the writer in presenting the theme of war?**

Ben Elton presents war as something really bad in this extract. This is done by making the location, the trenches, seem really horrible and the people who are in it are seen as desperate and unhappy. The first voice we hear is described to have 'cried' which makes it sound desperate and unhappy.

The language Elton uses also adds a feeling of depression such as 'beast of burden' with the alliteration making it sound like the carrying of a heavy burden is hard. He is described as a 'pack mule' which makes him seem like a donkey – man has become an animal. This is what war does to him. This is a depressing thought, as we start to become less human.

Lots of exclamations are used such as 'Man in the mud!' and '…for God's sake!' which shows how close the men are to dying – the desperation is shown by the exclamations.

*Annotations (right margin):*

- Overall evaluation
- Specific example given with a quotation and explanation of the effect and how this adds to the theme
- Another good example of a point being made with supporting quotation and explanation of the effect
- A further example of a technique – a man described as a pack mule, a supporting quotation and then an explanation of it

3 Write annotations for the last paragraph of this answer yourself.

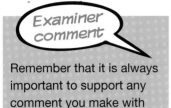

**4** Write your own notes on the last six lines of the extract, with a partner, picking out how the writer presents the scene and what he is saying about war. Try to come up with four separate points to discuss and four supporting quotations. How successful is the writer here?

When a writer presents a theme they may begin by giving a general view, establishing an appropriate mood.

Read the following extract from the beginning of *A Greyhound of A Girl* by Roddy Doyle.

Mary O'Hara was walking up her street, to the house she lived in with her parents and her brothers. The school bus had dropped her at the corner, at the bottom of the hill. The street was long, straight, and quite steep, and there were huge old chestnut trees growing all along both sides. It was raining, but Mary wasn't getting very wet, because the leaves and branches were like a roof above her. Anyway, rain and getting wet were things that worried adults, but not Mary – or anyone else under the age of twenty-one. Mary was twelve. She'd be twelve for another eight months. Then she'd be what she already felt she was – a teenager.

She came home at the same time most days, and she usually came home with her best friend, Ava. But today was different, because Ava wasn't with Mary. Ava had moved to another part of Dublin the day before, with her family. Today, some of the neighbours looked out their windows and saw Mary, alone. They knew all about it, of course. These were people who looked out windows. They'd seen the removals lorry outside Ava's house. They'd seen Mary and Ava hug each other, and they'd seen Ava get into their car and follow the removals lorry.

As the car moved slowly up the street, they'd seen Mary wave, and run into her house. They might have heard the front door slam. They might have heard Mary's feet charging up the stairs, and the springs under Mary's mattress groan when she fell facedown on the bed. They probably didn't hear her crying, and they definitely didn't hear the softer sound of the bedsprings a little later when Mary realized that, although she was heartbroken, she was also starving. So she got up and went downstairs to the kitchen and ate until her face was stiff.

Roddy Doyle, *A Greyhound of A Girl* (2012)

5 Explain what the main theme is here.
6 Say how successfully the writer has developed this theme. To do this, consider:

- how the narrator sets the scene
- how Mary's feelings are presented
- how the narrator presents Mary
- what makes her feel this way.

## 5 Setting and atmosphere

Writers normally set the scene of their story early on so you can picture it and feel the atmosphere. They then add extra detail as the story progresses.

## Practising for success

Read this extract in which the narrator, Anne, a teenage girl, has been left alone in her countryside home after a nuclear war has destroyed most of the country.

> I am afraid.
>
> Someone is coming.
>
> That is, I think someone is coming, though I am not sure and I pray that I am wrong. I went into the church and prayed all this morning. I sprinkled water in front of the altar, and put some flowers on it, violets and dogwood.
>
> But there is smoke. For three days there has been smoke, not like the time before. That time, last year, it rose in a great cloud a long way away, and stayed in the sky for two weeks. A forest fire in the dead woods, and then it rained and the smoke stopped. But this time it is a thin column, like a pole, not very high.
>
> And the column has come three times, each time in the late afternoon. At night I cannot see it, and in the morning, it is gone. But each afternoon it comes again, and it is nearer. At first it was behind Claypole Ridge, and I could see only the top of it, the smallest smudge. I thought it was a cloud, except that it was too grey, the wrong colour, and then I thought: there are no clouds anywhere else. I got the binoculars and saw that it was narrow and straight; it was smoke from a small fire. When we used to go in the truck, Claypole Ridge was fifteen miles, though it looks closer, and the smoke was coming from behind that.
>
> Robert O'Brien, *Z for Zachariah* (1974)

- How is the mood created at the start?
- What details are most significant in the extract?
- What atmosphere do the details and language create?
- Notice how the writer uses lots of short sentences and short paragraphs. What effect do they have?
- What might happen next? Support your ideas with reference to the source.

## ACTIVITY 1

See how a Grade 5 student writes about the effectiveness of the setting:

1 The student picks out the technique of one-sentence paragraphs and shows the effect – fear. There is no quotation used, however.

O'Brien uses short, one-sentence paragraphs at the start to emphasise the fear of the female character. We get the feeling that there is tension in the air. 'Smoke' is repeated in the third paragraph showing that this is the evidence that someone is coming, or a way to convince herself that someone is coming. It also gives the reader a reason for her fear.

We are then given the description of the other smoke – maybe it was a big bomb going off? Or a huge fire. We are kept guessing. The smoke now is compared to then and this time it is minor, just 'a thin column like a pole' with the simile making it seem slightly threatening, as a pole is hard and can be used to hurt people.

The smoke is described as a 'smudge' like it is nothing really big, but then it becomes more real and is 'smoke from a small fire'. This shows the reader that whoever is there is getting closer and we have the anticipation of what will happen when or if they meet.

2

3

4

5

**1** Offer annotations for the numbered points, saying what is good or needs to be improved in each case. The first one has been done for you.

**Boost your grade** ⬆

Often, writers rely heavily on their use of descriptive language to create an atmosphere.

This extract, set in the 1960s, describes the bleak morning atmosphere in the bedroom of Billy Casper, a very poor boy from Barnsley in Yorkshire.

> There were no curtains up. The window was a hard edged block the colour of the night sky. Inside the bedroom the darkness was of a gritty texture. The wardrobe and bed were blurred shapes in the darkness. Silence.
>
> Billy moved over, towards the outside of the bed. Jud, his brother, moved with him, leaving one half of the bed empty. He snorted and rubbed his nose. Billy whimpered. They settled. Wind whipped the window and swept along the wall outside.
>
> Billy turned over. Jud followed him and cough-coughed into his neck. Billy pulled the blankets up round his ears and wiped his neck with them. Most of the bed was now empty, and the unoccupied space quickly cooled. Silence. Then the alarm rang. The noise brought Billy upright, feeling for it in the darkness, eyes shut tight. Jud groaned and hunched back across the cold sheet. He reached down the side of the bed and knocked the clock over, grabbed for it, and knocked it further away.
>
> 'Come here, you bloody thing.'
>
> He stretched down and grabbed it with both hands. The glass lay curved in one palm, while the fingers of his other hand fumbled amongst the knobs and levers at the back. He found the lever and the noise stopped. Then he coiled back into the bed and left the clock lying on its back.
>
> 'The bloody thing.'

Barry Hines, *A Kestrel for a Knave* (1968)

1 What effect does using a number of short sentences in the first paragraph have on the reader?

2 What is the purpose of writing the word 'Silence' as a one-word sentence?

3 Look at the line: 'Wind whipped the window and swept along the wall outside.' What feeling does this create, and how?

4 What atmosphere is created through this extract? How is it achieved? How successful is the writer?

This is part of a Grade 3 response to the final question. How would you improve it?

> The atmosphere is horrible. The writer makes Billy's life seem grim, because he has to share a bed with his brother. And his brother swears. Nobody gets up when the alarm goes off and the clock is on the floor, not on a table, so the house doesn't have proper furniture. The weather is bad too. So it's not good either in the house or outside – 'The darkness was of a gritty texture'...

## Test yourself

Read the passage and then answer this exam-style question.

**The writer creates a bleak but quite humorous picture of his early childhood. To what extent do you agree?**

In your response, you should:

- write about your own impressions of his childhood
- evaluate how the writer has created these impressions
- support your opinions with quotations from the source.

The passage is from an autobiography by Frank McCourt about his own poor childhood in New York and then Ireland.

My father and mother should have stayed in New York where they met and married and where I was born. Instead, they returned to Ireland when I was four, my brother, Malachy, three, the twins, Oliver and Eugene, barely one, and my sister, Margaret, dead and gone.

When I look back on my childhood I wonder how I survived at all. It was, of course, a miserable childhood: the happy childhood is hardly worth your while. Worse than the ordinary miserable childhood is the miserable Irish childhood, and worse yet is the miserable Irish Catholic childhood.

People everywhere brag and whimper about the woes of their early years, but nothing can compare with the Irish version: the poverty; the shiftless **loquacious** alcoholic father; the **pious** defeated mother moaning by the fire; pompous priests; bullying schoolmasters; the English and the terrible things they did to us for eight hundred long years. Above all – we were wet.

**loquacious** means to talk a lot

**pious** is being a very good, religious person

**cacophony** is a loud noise

**consumptive** is someone with 'consumption': a term for the often fatal disease tuberculosis

**Benediction** is a short service that Catholics hold for a blessing from God

Out in the Atlantic Ocean great sheets of rain gathered to drift slowly up the River Shannon and settle forever in Limerick. The rain dampened the city from the Feast of the Circumcision to New Year's Eve. It created a **cacophony** of hacking coughs, bronchial rattles, asthmatic wheezes, **consumptive** croaks. It turned noses into fountains, lungs into bacterial sponges. It provoked cures galore; to ease the catarrh you boiled onions in milk blackened with pepper; for the congested passages you made a paste of boiled flour and nettles, wrapped it in a rag, and slapped it, sizzling, on the chest.

From October to April the walls of Limerick glistened with the damp. Clothes never dried: tweed and woollen coats housed living things, sometimes sprouted mysterious vegetations. In pubs, steam rose from damp bodies and garments to be inhaled with cigarette and pipe smoke laced with the stale fumes of spilled beer and whiskey.

The rain drove us into the church – our refuge, our strength, our only dry place. At Mass, **Benediction**, we huddled in great damp clumps, dozing through priest drone, while steam rose again from our clothes to mingle with the sweetness of incense, flowers and candles.

Limerick gained a reputation for **piety**, but we knew it was only the rain.

Frank McCourt, *Angela's Ashes* (1996)

### What you have learned

**In this unit you have learned to write about, explain and evaluate:**
- the importance of what someone looks like and how they act
- what you find out about characters from what they say and what they do
- how writers present relationships
- how writers explore themes
- how writers use settings.

# Paper 2, Section A

## What you have to do...

Paper 2, Section A is challenging because you have to deal with two sources on a similar subject – one from the nineteenth century and one from the twentieth or twenty-first century. They will be non-fiction, so they might be diary entries, letters, articles, reports or speeches.

As with Paper 1, Section A, there are four questions, with 40 marks available.

You are advised to spend approximately one hour on the section, reading the sources and answering the questions. If you commit approximately 15 minutes to reading the sources carefully, that will leave you 45 minutes to write your answers.

The questions will be as follows:

| Q1 | 4 marks | You will be given eight statements about one of the sources: you have to say which four are true. |
| --- | --- | --- |
| Q2 | 8 marks | You will need to write about both sources and summarise some differences or similarities. |
| Q3 | 12 marks | Focusing on just one of the sources, you will have to say how the writer has used language for effect. |
| Q4 | 16 marks | Again, you have to consider both sources and write about a point of comparison – for example, the attitude of the writers towards their subject. In your answer, you will have to include the methods they use. |

As with Paper 1, Section A, there are no marks for your technical accuracy, but you should try to be as accurate as possible, to help the examiner understand your ideas.

# Q1 Finding what is true

### In this unit you will:
⇨ learn the differences between facts, false facts and opinions
⇨ identify facts, false facts and opinions in non-fiction texts
⇨ think about what is implied in a text as well as what is stated clearly.

## What this unit involves

This unit deals with Paper 2, Question 1.

You will have to read a piece of non-fiction and then select four statements about the writing that are true, from a list of eight statements. The section of text you have to deal with will be at the start of the extract.

There are 4 marks for this question, which you need to complete in about 4 minutes.

## 1 Identifying facts, opinions and false facts

**A fact** is something that is true and can be proved. In the pieces of writing below the facts are highlighted in blue.

As I write this, Queen Elizabeth is the Queen of England. She has been queen for over 60 years. She was born on 21 April 1926 and became queen in 1952. She has four children. Her eldest son, Prince Charles, is next in line to the throne.

London hosted the Olympics in 2012. The Olympics were a triumph for Britain. There were over 200 countries participating. There were also over 10,000 athletes who took part, in over 300 events. The opening ceremony was watched by an estimated audience of 900 million worldwide.

## Practising for success

### ACTIVITY 1

1 With a partner, write down three facts about your school or college.
2 Now read the report on page 59, which is taken from the *Guardian* newspaper.
   List four facts that you can find in the report.

# Clear differences between organic and non-organic food, study finds

## Research is first to find wide-ranging differences between organic and conventional fruits, vegetables and cereals

*Damian Carrington and George Arnett*

Organic food has more of the antioxidant compounds linked to better health than regular food, and lower levels of toxic metals and pesticides, according to the most comprehensive scientific analysis to date.

The international team behind the work suggests that switching to organic fruit and vegetables could give the same benefits as adding one or two portions of the recommended "five a day".

The team, led by Prof Carlo Leifert at Newcastle University, concludes that there are "statistically significant, meaningful" differences, with a range of **antioxidants**

being "substantially higher" – between 19% and 69% – in organic food. It is the first study to demonstrate clear and wide-ranging differences between organic and conventional fruits, vegetables and cereals.

**antioxidants** are nutrients that help the body to fight disease. An antioxidant compound is an essential part of a healthy balanced diet

Damian Carrington and George Arnett, the *Guardian* (2014)

**An opinion** is a belief or judgement that cannot be proven. For example:

*Rhianna is the best singer in the world. I think she has an amazing voice and is extremely talented.*

*Fried eggs taste better than boiled eggs. Boiled eggs smell awful and take ages to cook. I love eating fried-egg sandwiches.*

*Summer is an awful time of year. It gets far too hot. There are insects crawling about everywhere and you can get burnt easily. I don't understand why anyone likes summer. I hate it.*

## ACTIVITY 2

**1** With a partner, write down four opinions about your school or college.

**2** Now read the *Guardian* article again. List four opinions in the article.

A **false fact** is a statement that appears to be true, but isn't. For example:

*The earth is flat.*

*King James is the current ruler of England.*

*There are 28 days in the month of January.*

## ACTIVITY 3

Read the article below.

### Are fathers better at bedtime stories than mothers?

I was seven years old when my grandfather and I would sit together in the front room of his terraced house in Manchester. I spent many hours watching him sip tea and listen to him reciting the poems that he had learned at school when he himself had been a child.

Grandad Dean's favourite poem was 'If' by Rudyard Kipling. "If you can fill the unforgiving minute, with sixty seconds' worth of distance run …"

At the time I preferred watching television to listening to Tennyson's 'The Charge of the Light Brigade'. However, unknown to my grandfather, his poetry recitals did have a lasting impact on me.

I was very lucky to have a grandfather with such a love of poetry. He shared his passion of words with me from a young age. I have been so influenced by him that I now recite poetry to my own daughters, Poppy and Maya, who are aged four and eight respectively.

1 Which statements from the following list are true, and which ones are false?
   a) The writer's grandfather was called Dean.
   b) The writer preferred watching TV to listening to someone read to him.
   c) The writer has two daughters.
   d) The writer dislikes reading to his daughters.
   e) The writer's daughters are four and eight years old.
   f) The writer's grandfather also liked watching television.
   g) Grandad Dean only drank tea.
   h) The writer loved his grandfather.
2 With a partner, write down four false facts about your school or college.

Now read the article.

**3** List four facts and four opinions in the article. In each case, explain why they are facts or opinions.

## Richard III: Website details history of king found under Leicester car park

Leicester Cathedral has launched a Richard III website today to coincide with the one-year anniversary of the positive identification of the king.

On February 4 last year, the University of Leicester identified a set of human remains found at the New Street car park as those of King Richard III.

A site dedicated to the **Plantagenet** monarch went live at midnight last night with the aim of boosting support for the city's **reinterment** plans.

It outlines the story of the medieval monarch — his life, death and discovery — and his 500-year connection to the city and county.

It is also aimed at highlighting the importance of why Richard III should be laid to rest in Leicester.

Bishop Tim Stevens said "The story of the king in a car park has become part of the life of our city and part of the story of our nation.

"Now we look forward to welcoming people from around the world to become part of our shared story. This new website presents Richard's story clearly once again and begins the next chapter — our task of laying the king to rest with dignity and honour."

The website also features "facts and fictions" about the former King of England, and includes a section where people can donate towards the cost of the reinterment.

There is also a video showing Richard's link to Leicester and explaining some of the ideas behind the reinterment.

City mayor Peter Soulsby said Leicester Cathedral is the only fitting place for the remains to be reinterred.

He said: "The cathedral has demonstrated very clearly why Leicester is the right location for the final resting place."

www.leicestermercury.co.uk

The House of **Plantagenet** held the English throne from the accession of Henry II in 1154 to the death of Richard III in 1485

**reinterment** – reburial

## 2 Distinguishing between facts, false facts and opinions

In order to be successful in the examination, you will need to be able to sort out the true facts from the false ones and the opinions.

## Practising for success

Read the following extract from the Victoria and Albert Museum website. It is an article about an exhibition on the Indian film industry that took place in 2002. The Indian film industry is called Bollywood.

| Home | Visiting | Explore | Support us | Learning | What's on | Shop | Membership | Blog |

Search 🔍

### Cinema India: The Art of Bollywood

26th June – 6th October 2002

*Featuring works from pre-independent India to the present day, this exhibition charted the historical, political and cultural changes experienced by the country, as seen through the eyes of the Indian film industry.*

*The exhibition brought together some of the most remarkable examples of Indian cinema art, from large-scale hoardings and posters to photo cards, booklets and original film trailers. Posters from many classic films were represented: the Oscar nominated epic 'Mother India', 'Sholay' (with its distinctive and influential typography) and recent blockbusters such as 'Lagaan' and 'K3G'.*

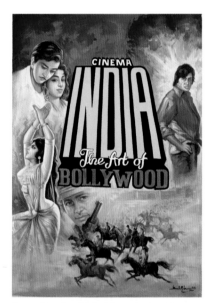

Film hoarding by Balkrishna Arts, oil on canvas, India, 2002, Museum no. IS.115-2002

Victoria and Albert Museum, London (2002)

### ACTIVITY 1

**1** Which four statements from the following list are true about the extract?

**a)** The exhibition looked at the Indian film industry from before independence to the century.

**b)** The exhibition was about the American film industry.

**c)** The exhibition took place in 2001.

**d)** The exhibition gave the public the opportunity to watch an Indian film.

**e)** Original film trailers were shown at the exhibition.

**f)** The film *Mother India* was nominated for an Oscar.

**g)** The film *K3G* won an Oscar.

**h)** One of the more recent film posters was for a film called *Lagaan*.

To decide which statements are true, use this approach:

Read each statement individually.

*The exhibition looked at the Indian film industry from before independence to the twenty-first century.*

Examiner comment

Having a system that you use each time to identify the facts is recommended.

Read the source provided and try to find words or phrases that are in the statement and that are also in the source (in the exam you would highlight it). In this statement the significant phrase is the Indian film industry from before independence to 2002.

Now read the statement again, and then the sentence that you have identified.

*The exhibition looked at the Indian film industry from before independence to the century.*

**Featuring works from pre-independent India to the present day ...**

Compare the statement with the sentence in the source. Is the statement true or false?

Below is another extract from the Victoria and Albert Museum museum website.

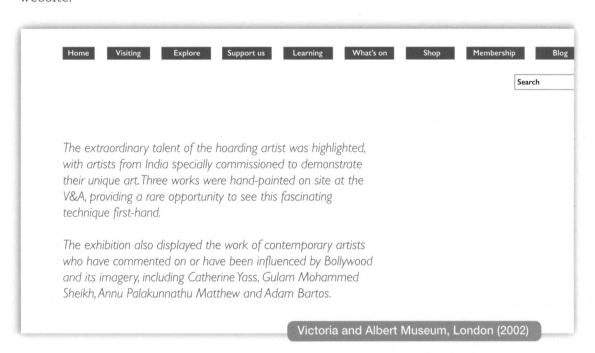

| Home | Visiting | Explore | Support us | Learning | What's on | Shop | Membership | Blog |

Search

*The extraordinary talent of the hoarding artist was highlighted, with artists from India specially commissioned to demonstrate their unique art. Three works were hand-painted on site at the V&A, providing a rare opportunity to see this fascinating technique first-hand.*

*The exhibition also displayed the work of contemporary artists who have commented on or have been influenced by Bollywood and its imagery, including Catherine Yass, Gulam Mohammed Sheikh, Annu Palakunnathu Matthew and Adam Bartos.*

Victoria and Albert Museum, London (2002)

**2** Which statements from the following list are true, and which are false?
  **a)** There was a play staged at the exhibition.
  **b)** Artists from India were commissioned to do more paintings.
  **c)** Four works of art were painted at the museum.
  **d)** It is quite rare to see artists painting hoardings.
  **e)** Gulam Mohammed Sheikh's work had been influenced by Bollywood.
  **f)** A female artist called Catherine Yass had work on display.
  **g)** There was no work by modern artists on display.
  **h)** One of the artists who had work on display was Adam Singh.

A student thought the following answers were true:

> a) There was a play staged at the exhibition.
> d) It is quite rare to see artists painting hoardings.
> f) A female artist called Catherine Yass had work on display.
> g) There was no work by modern artists on display.

**Discussion points**

**3** With a partner, look at each statement and discuss why the student would have thought that each of these answers was true.

The same student thought that the following answers were false:

> b) Artists from India were commissioned to do more paintings.
> c) Four works of art were painted at the museum.
> e) Gulam Mohammed Sheikh's work had been influenced by Bollywood.
> h) One of the artists who had work on display was Adam Singh.

**4** With a partner, look at each statement and discuss why the student would have thought that each of these answers was false.

As a reminder…

**5** What four things should you do before answering Question 1 in the exam?

**6** Write down a fact, opinion and false fact about the person sitting next to you.

## Test yourself

Read the extract below which is taken from *Red Dust*, a piece of travel writing by Ma Jian. In this extract, the narrator is searching for a lake so that he can get some water and find people to save him.

After an hour's descent I reach the desert. Sweat pours from my body and evaporates in seconds. My water is half-finished, and the lake has sunk from view. I must rely on my compass from now on. The sun is still overhead. As I breathe the hot air in and out, my mouth becomes as dry as dust. The compass in my hand burns like the gravel underfoot. The **dry noodles** have reached my stomach and seem to be sucking the moisture from my blood. I long to reach the shore of the lake and plunge my head in its cool water. For brief moments, refracted through the heat waves on the right, I see villages, moving trucks, or a sweep of marsh. If I didn't have a compass, I might be tempted to walk straight into the mirage. Four or five hours go by. At last I see clumps of weed rise from the

**dry noodles,** the food that the narrator ate at the start of his journey

gravel. The land starts to dip. I check the compass. **Sugan** should be right in front of me now, but all I see is the wide stony plain.

Suddenly it dawns on me that distances can be deceptive in the transparent atmosphere of the desert. The lake that from the pass seemed so near could be a hundred kilometres away. After all, what looked like a tiny blue spot is in fact a huge lake. It is too late to turn back now though – my bottle is empty. I have no choice but to keep walking towards the water. Where there is water there are people, and where there are people there is life. There is no other path I can take.

As the sun sinks to the west, the lake reappears at last. It is not a lake exactly, just a line of grey slightly brighter than the desert stones, not wavering in the heat haze this time, but lying still at the edge of the sky. I am on course, but my legs can barely hold. There is camel-thorn underfoot now and the earth is covered with a thick saline crust. The sun sinks slowly below me, then reddens and disappears.

Ma Jian, *Red Dust* (2002)

Write down four statements below which you think are **true**.
Choose a maximum of four statements.

{ **Sugan** is a lake in north-west China }

  a) It took the narrator an hour to reach the desert.
  b) The narrator feels very cold.
  c) The narrator has to use a compass to find his way.
  d) A day passes before the land starts to dip.
  e) Reaching Sugan takes longer than the narrator expected.
  f) The narrator has plenty of water.
  g) The narrator's legs are weak.
  h) By the end of the extract it is still light.

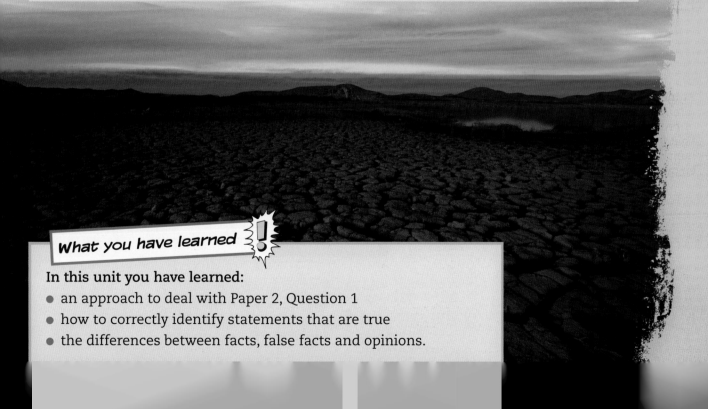

## What you have learned !

In this unit you have learned:
- an approach to deal with Paper 2, Question 1
- how to correctly identify statements that are true
- the differences between facts, false facts and opinions.

# Q2 Dealing with two texts and summarising

## What this unit involves

This unit deals with Paper 2, Question 2. You will have to write a summary of the differences or similarities between the content of the two non-fiction texts: possibly, you will have to write about the people in them, or the settings or the themes.

There are 8 marks for this question and you will need to answer it in 8 or 9 minutes.

## 1 Locating the relevant information

Before coming to this question, you will already have read the sources. You should therefore know what they are all about!

You will, though, have to find information in them. Some might be explicit; some might be implicit.

### Key terms

**Explicit:** what is clearly stated

**Implicit:** what is suggested

## Practising for success

Here, a campaigner against torture gives his views:

> Beatings. Rape. Electric shocks. Whipping. Burning. Humiliation. Sleep deprivation. Water torture. Long hours in contorted positions. Pincers. Drugs. Dogs. In the course of **Amnesty's** work this year, we recorded at least 27 different torture methods still being used today.
>
> Every day, in every region of the world, unimaginable horrors are a reality for countless men, women and children.
>
> Torture is barbaric and inhumane. Torture can never be justified. Torture poisons the rule of law, replacing it with terror. No one is safe when governments allow its use.
>
> Salil Shetty, 'Now Stop It', *The Amnesty Magazine* (2014)

**Amnesty** is Amnesty International, a movement of 7 million people who fight for a world where human rights can be enjoyed by all

## ACTIVITY 1

**1** What forms of torture are mentioned?

**2** What do we learn about torture here?

The answers to both these questions are straightforward: the information is listed for us.

Of course, the task in the examination will be more complex.

Read this extract:

> I started writing a play earlier this year based around a family reunion at Christmas and I got stuck. Not with the creation of the characters but with the plot. The characters were no real problem because I did what I always do and plundered the family vaults and my web of friends and acquaintances for eccentric and/or lustful uncles, **neurotic** cousins, **bawdy** grandads and forgetful aunts. It's a lot easier writing about people you know than it is trying to make up characters out of thin air, though you generally don't use the whole person in case you get sued or written out of various wills.
>
> Mike Harding, 'Enter an Egyptian Doctor covered in cat poo', *Hypnotising the Cat* (1995)

**neurotic** means stressed out

**bawdy** means to make vulgar jokes

**3** What are the two main sources the writer uses when he has to invent characters?

**4** Why does the writer have to be careful not to upset anyone?

In this case, it was a matter of reading through and finding the relevant section of the source, to locate the explicit information you needed.

There is, though, implicit information in this source too. If you were asked:

*'What do you learn about the writer here?'*

that would be harder.

**5** What explicit information can you find about him?

**6** What is also suggested about him? What sort of person is he?

Copy and complete the table below, explaining what the writer is like.

| WHAT HE WRITES | WHAT THIS SUGGESTS ABOUT HIM |
| --- | --- |
| I … plundered the family vaults | He uses people for his own ends/he has a wealth of interesting acquaintances |
| He has eccentric and/or lustful uncles, neurotic cousins, bawdy grandads and forgetful aunts | |
| you generally don't use the whole person in case you get sued or written out of various wills | |

One of the sources you will be dealing with will have been written in the 19th century.

This was written by American Mark Twain.

transient means temporary

**Minstrel shows** were touring variety shows – at that time, they would be made up of African-Americans and were often mocking and racist in tone

**clerks** are office workers

When I was a boy, there was but one permanent ambition among my comrades in our village on the West bank of the Mississippi River. That was, to be a steamboatman. We had **transient** ambitions of other sorts, but they were only transient. When a circus came and went, it left us all burning to become clowns; the first **minstrel show** that came to our section left us all suffering to try that kind of life; now and then we had a hope that if we lived and were good, God would permit us to be pirates. These ambitions faded out, each in its turn; but the ambition to be a steamboatman always remained.

After all these years, I can picture that old time to myself now, just as it was then: the white town drowsing in the sunshine of a summer's morning; the streets empty, or pretty near so; one or two **clerks** sitting in front of the Water Street stores, with their chairs tilted back against the wall, chins on breasts, hats slouched over their faces, asleep; a sow and a litter of pigs loafing along the sidewalk; the fragrant town drunkard asleep…

Mark Twain, 'Old Times on the Mississippi', *Atlantic Monthly* (1875)

7 What were Mark Twain's ambitions when he was young?

8 What did he want to become more than anything?

If you were asked what sort of place the writer lived in, you would need to consider:

- the details we are given – the explicit information
- what is suggested by them – the implicit information: what is being suggested or implied.

9 List the details in the extract that give a picture of the place.

10 Look carefully at the language used to describe the place. What do the following words and phrases suggest?

- *white town*
- *drowsing in the sunshine*
- *chairs tilted back… chins on breasts… hats slouched over their faces, asleep*

- *pigs loafing along the sidewalk*
- *fragrant town drunkard*

Now put all your ideas together to answer the following question:

**11** What do we learn about Twain's life when he was a boy?

**1** Look at how this student wrote about Mark Twain's life when he was a boy and respond to the questions in the annotations:

Could this have been more precise?

What other detail should have been included here?

What might Twain be suggesting about the place?

> Mark Twain was a boy in America. When he was young he wanted to be lots of things like a clown but most of all he wanted to be a steamboatman. He lived in a place that was white and nothing much seemed to happen. There were pigs in the street and no one seemed to mind. The town had only one drunk and he was asleep all the time.

Not very precise: but what point could be made about the drunk?

Is there anything else that could have been added to this point?

Interprets the atmosphere but how could the idea have been supported?

Again, offers implicit understanding – but could other detail have been added? Explain

The response is Grade 3 standard, because there is some inference and there are appropriate references to the text.

**2** Read the next response, which is clearly better. Explain why it is better and what it does well.

> We get a clear picture of what Mark Twain's life was like. He had lots of dreams when he was a boy. He sometimes wanted to be a clown or a minstrel or a pirate. However, all those ideas faded and finally he just wanted to be a steamboatman. Perhaps this was because he lived on the Mississippi River.
>
> The town he lived in seems very sleepy. The clerks are asleep and the 'fragrant town drunkard' is asleep too. Everything seems quiet: the town is 'drowsing', the streets are 'empty', the clerks have stopped work and are sitting with their chairs back, 'chins on breasts, hats slouched over their faces'. It all sounds as if nothing is going on at all. Obviously it is a very backward place too, because the pigs wander where they want in the street.

**3** Are there any ways even this Grade 5 answer could be improved still further?

# 2 How to summarise

The question you must answer will ask you to summarise information, not just list it. That means you have to:

- find the relevant points
- explain them in your own words
- support them with quotations, to prove what you say.

## Practising for success

Read this extract from a newspaper article commenting on London today:

> provincial means away from the capital city

A restaurant in a **provincial** city. Around the table, people I know only a little. Menus discussed, wine ordered, weather slagged off, the talk has turned – as it inevitably does these days – to London. 'The public transport!' moans one. 'So awful, and so expensive.' Another talks indignantly of the Russians who've 'taken over' Mayfair, as if Berkeley Square had been previously inhabited by the working poor. 'I'm glad to be out of it,' says the man opposite. 'Me, too,' says the woman to his left. On and on it goes until, finally, they look at me: 'Do you live in central London?' The question is asked in much the same tone as you might enquire of a beautician how she feels about waxing the backsides of her hairy male clients. 'Yes, I do.' I tell them, my voice deliberately loud. The temptation to add 'So yah, boo, sucks to you!' is powerfully strong.

I can't help it. I like London, for all its faults. I'm happy that for the time being I can afford to live there.

Rachel Cooke, the *Observer* (2014)

### ACTIVITY 1

**1** What do the people in the extract think about London? Summarise their views.

List:
- the criticisms, and the attitude of the people around the table towards London
- the writer's opinion.

To summarise the thoughts, you need to express the ideas in a new way, bringing them together but also showing where you got them from. So, a Grade 5 student wrote:

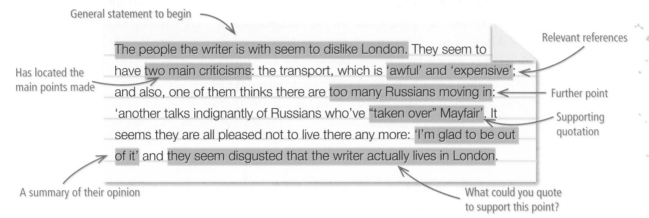

General statement to begin

Has located the main points made

The people the writer is with seem to dislike London. They seem to have two main criticisms: the transport, which is 'awful' and 'expensive'; and also, one of them thinks there are too many Russians moving in: 'another talks indignantly of Russians who've "taken over" Mayfair'. It seems they are all pleased not to live there any more: 'I'm glad to be out of it' and they seem disgusted that the writer actually lives in London.

Relevant references

Further point

Supporting quotation

A summary of their opinion

What could you quote to support this point?

**2** Write a response of your own in response to this question:

What is the writer's opinion of London and what is her opinion of these people?

**Examiner comments**

As a general rule, try to range across the text: in the examination, you might well find that some of the more important material occurs towards the end. If you have used your 15 minutes of reading time well, you should have some knowledge of where to find what you need.

You might be faced with sources that seem far removed from modern life. In that case, if you encounter words or phrases with which you are unfamiliar, try to just read through them, because hopefully the remainder of the source will make sense to you.

This extract deals with the survivors of a shipwreck in the Pacific Ocean on 20 November 1820. Their whaling ship was sunk by a giant whale and they had to set out for land in smaller boats.

> Twenty men set out in open whaleboats for the coast of South America 2000 miles away. They had bread, water and some Galapagos turtles. Although they were at the time no great distance from Tahiti, they were ignorant of the temper of the natives and feared cannibalism.
>
> Their first extreme sufferings commenced a week later when they made the mistake of eating, in order to make their supply last, some bread which had got soaked by the sea's wash. To alleviate the thirst which followed, they killed turtle for its blood. The sight revolted the stomachs of the men.
>
> In the first weeks of December their lips began to crack and swell, and a glutinous saliva collected in the mouth, intolerable to the taste.

Their bodies commenced to waste away, and possessed so little strength they had to assist each other in performing some of the body's weakest functions. Barnacles collected on the ships' bottoms and they tore them off for food. A few flying fish struck their sails, fell into the boats and were swallowed raw.

Already one of the men had died, Matthew Joy, second mate. He had been buried at sea on 10 January. When Charles Shorter died on 23 January, his body was shared among the men and eaten. Two days more and Lawson Thomas died and was eaten. Again two days and Isaak Shepherd died and was eaten…

Charles Olson, *Call Me Ishmail* (1947)

**3** Write down any words or phrases you do not immediately understand.

**4** Even without understanding everything perfectly, can you still follow what happens?

**5** Share your list with a friend. Together, can you make sense of the whole text?

**Task:** Write a summary of what you know about the sailors.

This is only a practice, so you can't underline sections of the source – instead you will be making notes.

In the examination, it is acceptable to underline and annotate the exam paper itself. Indeed, that approach is recommended, to help you deal with the sources and identify and write about the relevant sections.

Work through each paragraph, saying what happened – and remembering to use your own words – apart from when you are including names of people or the names of things for which there is not really an alternative (e.g. saliva).

For example:

> Para 1: 20 men in whaleboats: South America 2000 miles / only limited supplies / Tahiti close but might have had cannibals there
> Para 2: …
> Para 3: …

Your task is always to offer a response which is much shorter than the original, but which has the main points and includes supporting evidence.

**6** Write your response.

**Boost your grade** ⬆

This is a promising Grade 4 response:

> The sailors had a terrible time. They were adrift in whaleboats and had to sail to South America, which was 2000 miles away. They didn't have much to eat or drink and couldn't go to Tahiti in case the locals ate them! **But at least they must have known where they were.** They made a mistake and ate bread soaked in seawater, which made them thirsty, so they killed a turtle for its blood, but that made them sick. Their mouths got nasty and swollen and they had a terrible taste in them. It seems as if they had to help each other go to the toilet and they had to eat barnacles and flying fish. **Then they must have got desperate** because they had to start eating each other.

← Inference

← Further inference

What is missing from the response? List the things you would add.

## 3 Linking two texts

So far, we have been practising the basic skills you will need to answer Question 2 on Paper 2. However, you will have to deal with two sources at once. This means having to:

● identify the key information in both sources
● make links between the sources.

When you are in the exam, it will help you to underline the relevant details in the sources. Then you have to write about them effectively. You are expected to 'demonstrate clear connections between them'.

## Practising for success

We are going to begin by looking at another two extracts that deal with London.

### Source A
That great foul city of London there…
rattling, growling, smoking, stinking…
a ghastly heap of fermenting brickwork,
pouring out poison at every pore.

John Ruskin (19th century)

## Source B

I do like the Underground. There's something surreal about plunging into the bowels of the earth to catch a train. It's a little world of its own down there, with its own strange winds and weather systems, its own eerie noises and oily smells. Even when you've descended so far into the earth that you've lost your bearings utterly and wouldn't be in the least surprised to pass a troop of blackened miners coming off shift, there's always the rumble and tremble of a train passing somewhere on an unknown line even further below. And it all happens in such orderly quiet: all these thousands of people passing on stairs and escalators, stepping on and off crowded trains, sliding off into the darkness with wobbling heads, and never speaking, like characters from Night of the Living Dead.

Bill Bryson, *Notes from a Small Island* (20th century)

### ACTIVITY 1

**1** What different impressions of London are presented in these extracts?

To deal with the question, you first have to work out what each writer thinks.

**a)** Find two words to describe Ruskin's attitude to London.

**b)** Decide what impression is being created in each of the following phrases and how that impression is created. Copy and complete the table.

| PHRASE | IMPLICATION ABOUT LONDON | HOW THE IMPRESSION IS CREATED |
|--------|--------------------------|-------------------------------|
| That great foul city of London there | It is huge, smelly and unhealthy | 'great' means big, not wonderful here / foul is emotive and suggests there is an unpleasant smell |
| Rattling, growling, smoking, stinking | | |
| A ghastly heap of fermenting brickwork, pouring out poison at every pore | | |

Now turn your attention to Bryson's extract.

**2** Which details could you use to make a direct comparison to Ruskin's ideas?

**3** Copy and complete these two lists, showing in what ways the impression created is the same, and in what ways it is different.

| SIMILARITIES | DIFFERENCES |
|---|---|
| Sounds, e.g. | Bryson likes London, Ruskin doesn't |
|  |  |
|  |  |

There are two methods you can use to make your comparison.

## Method 1

- Make a general statement of differences/similarities.
- Then work through the sources together, writing about the points of comparison as you go:
  - Ruskin believes … But Bryson is very different because …
  - Of course, Ruskin mentions … and so does Bryson, when he writes '…
- Summarise to finish (mentioning the main points of comparison you have worked through).

## Method 2

- Write about just one source (here, what Ruskin thinks of London).
- Then write about the other but make references back to the first source, including comparisons at this point.
- Summarise to finish.

This is part of a Grade 4 answer, using Method 1.

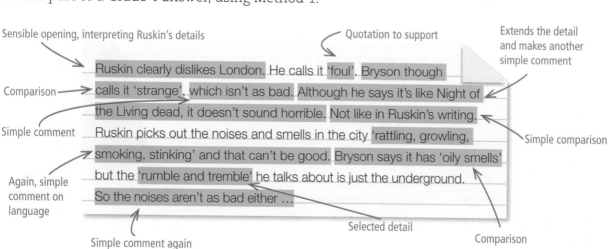

Sensible opening, interpreting Ruskin's details

Quotation to support

Extends the detail and makes another simple comment

Comparison

Simple comment

Again, simple comment on language

Simple comment again

Selected detail

Simple comparison

Comparison

Ruskin clearly dislikes London. He calls it 'foul'. Bryson though calls it 'strange', which isn't as bad. Although he says it's like Night of the Living dead, it doesn't sound horrible. Not like in Ruskin's writing. Ruskin picks out the noises and smells in the city 'rattling, growling, smoking, stinking' and that can't be good. Bryson says it has 'oily smells' but the 'rumble and tremble' he talks about is just the underground. So the noises aren't as bad either …

**Examiner comment**

If you decide to use Method 2, make sure you make the comparisons as you deal with the second source. Your mark will suffer if you simply write about the two sources without offering the required links between them.

**4** Improve this response listing the additional points or quotations you would insert and deciding what points you would add at the end.

Many students find it is easier to use Method 2.

Hopefully you now have all the ideas sorted out. Now, produce a full answer to the question (Question 1 on page 74), but using Method 2. Make sure you:

- give a detailed response to the short extracts from Ruskin
- include details from the whole of the text from Bryson
- use quotations throughout
- include what each writer is suggesting about London
- summarise the information, don't simply copy it
- make those essential comparisons
- sum up the different impressions in your final paragraph.

## Test yourself

Remember all you have learnt and complete the following task.

You need to refer to **Source A** and **Source B** for this question.

**Use details from both sources. Write a summary of the similarities and differences between the two nurses.**

### Source A

This is part of the story of Agnes Jones, a nurse who worked in the hospital for the poor in Liverpool but died of typhus fever that she caught there. It is from a letter written by Florence Nightingale in 1868.

One woman has died – a woman, attractive and rich, young and witty, yet a veiled and silent woman who trained herself in order to train others to walk in the footsteps of **Him** who went about doing good.

{ Him is Jesus }

She died as she had lived, at her post in one of the largest poorhouse infirmaries in this kingdom, the first in which trained nursing has been introduced. She is the pioneer of poorhouse nursing. I do not give her name. Were she alive, she would beg me not to. Of all human beings I have ever known, she was the most free from the desire of the praise of men. She preferred being unknown but to God; she did not let her left hand know what her right hand did.

In less than three years at that hospital, she achieved miracles. She had the gracefulness, the wit, the unfailing cheerfulness – qualities so remarkable but so much overlooked. As for the nurses, her influence with them was unbounded. They would have died for her, because they always felt that she cared for them, not merely as her workers, but for each one in herself. And she never knew that she was doing anything remarkable.

Florence Nightingale (19th century)

## Source B

This report is about a nurse who caught the deadly Ebola virus whilst helping those suffering with the disease in Sierra Leone.

# British nurse with Ebola virus has 'very good' chance of survival

*David Mabey from the London School of Hygiene and Tropical Medicine says the chances of British nurse William Pooley surviving the Ebola virus are "very good"*

DAVID MABEY, Professor of Communicable Diseases at the London School of Hygiene and Tropical Medicine, said that Nurse William Pooley who contracted Ebola while working in Sierra Leone has a "very good" chance of survival, adding that the risk of anyone else catching it from him are "zero".

Nurse Pooley, 29, contracted the deadly disease while working around the clock to help staff at an understaffed hospital in the west African country contain the outbreak.

He was transferred to the UK's only isolation ward – at the Royal Free Hospital – on Sunday, after being airlifted to RAF Northolt.

Despite catching the virus from the people he was trying to save, Mr Pooley reportedly told friends in Sierra Leone that he is determined to beat the disease, and vowed to return and help other victims after his recovery.

Speaking about the care the nurse would be receiving at the Royal Free, Mr Mabey added that as there are no cures or preventive medication available, doctors would be treating Mr Pooley's symptoms as they currently presented.

However, he added that it was a positive sign that Mr Pooley's symptoms had apparently been caught early.

There have so far been 2,615 confirmed cases and 1,427 deaths in the outbreak in Africa.

The virus is contracted through contact with an infected person's bodily fluid. Symptoms of the virus appear as a sudden onset of fever, headache, sore throat, intense weakness and muscle pain.

*The Telegraph (2014)*

## What you have learned !

In this unit you have learned to:
- find explicit and implicit information
- summarise sources
- compare sources, using different methods.

**In this unit you will learn how to analyse and write about:**

⇨ persuasive words and phrases writers have used

⇨ linguistic features and techniques

⇨ how persuasive techniques are used to influence the reader.

### What this unit involves

This unit deals with Paper 2, Question 3. You will have a question on how the writer has used persuasive language in a non-fiction text.

There are 12 marks for this question, so you can spend 12 or 13 minutes answering it.

## 1 Analysing language – an introduction

In Question 3, you need to be able to identify persuasive words and phrases and describe their effect. In this unit we'll be exploring how adjectives and emotive language are used in non-fiction.

## Practising for success

Read the piece of travel writing below and then answer the questions that follow.

---

**A cycling tour of Cuba: readers' travel writing competition**

*Steve Rocliffe won the journey category. On a cycle around west Cuba, he explores the byways of a country in transition*

{ papaya is an exotic fruit }

I only wanted a **papaya** but from the look of distress on the face of the roadside fruit-seller, I suspect I've asked for something rather different. It turns out that I have. "In Cuba, papaya means lady parts," says my guide, Andy, to my shame. "You must never, ever, say that word."

It was to be the first of several fruit stops — and almost as many cultural missteps — on a cycling adventure that promised to showcase a traditional side to this outpost of communism, one very different from Varadero, the island's main beach resort. Over five days, we would journey through the agricultural heartland of western Cuba, taking in the ancient landscapes of the Viñales region, the wilder beaches of the north coast and the forested slopes of the Sierra del Rosario mountain range, before hanging up our helmets in the hustle of Havana.

Steve Rocliffe, the *Guardian* (2014)

## Adjectives

**ACTIVITY 1**

1 The writer has used several **adjectives** to describe his cycling tour around Cuba. Copy and complete the table below, exploring what these adjectives suggest about the island. The first one has been done for you.

| ADJECTIVE | EFFECT |
|---|---|
| traditional side | The adjective 'traditional' suggests that the island is not modern. It implies that there are some old-fashioned parts to this country. |
| ancient landscapes | The adjective 'ancient' suggests... |
| wilder beaches | The adjective 'wilder' suggests... |

A student produced this Grade 4 standard response about the use of adjectives in the article.

> The writer, Rocliffe, uses lots of adjectives to describe his journey around Cuba. For example, he uses the adjective 'traditional' to show the reader that Cuba is still quite an old-fashioned country in many ways. He also uses adjectives such as 'ancient' and 'forested' to show us how beautiful different parts of Cuba are.

*Discussion point*

2 With a partner, discuss what is good about this paragraph and what could be improved.

3 Rewrite and extend the paragraph so that it gets a Grade 5.

## Emotive language

Emotive language is used extensively in persuasive writing: writers like to have an emotional impact on their readers.

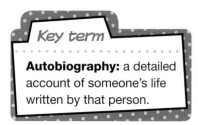

**Key term**

**Autobiography:** a detailed account of someone's life written by that person.

Read the extract below. It is from the **autobiography** of Mo Farah, a British runner. Some examples of emotive language have been highlighted.

Everyone is roaring me on. The noise is unbelievable. Like nothing I've ever heard before. The crowd is giving me a massive boost. I think about how many people are crammed inside the stadium — how many millions more are watching on TV at home, cheering me on. Willing me to win. None of the other guys out there on the track are getting this kind of support. Everyone is rooting for me. The noise gets louder and louder. The crowd is lifting me. Pushing me on through the pain, towards the finish line.

Mo Farah, *Twin Ambitions* (2013)

## ACTIVITY 2

1 Copy and complete the table below, explaining how Farah has used the emotive language highlighted above to emphasise the thrilling atmosphere inside the stadium. The first two have been done for you.

| EMOTIVE LANGUAGE | EFFECT |
|---|---|
| roaring me on | This highlights how loud the stadium is and how the crowd is fully supportive of the athlete. The verb 'roaring' also suggests that there is an exciting, powerful atmosphere in the stadium as lions usually roar. |
| giving me a massive boost | This implies that the support of the crowd is invaluable to Mo Farah and really helps him. The verb 'giving' suggests that the crowd are supporting him. |
| many millions more are watching on TV | |

A student wrote the following paragraph about the use of emotive language in the extract.

> Mo Farah uses lots of emotive language in the passage to show us how excited everyone is about his race. For example, he uses the verbs 'roaring', 'willing' and 'rooting'. These verbs show us that the crowd is behind him.

This extract comes from a Grade 4 response. The student was able to identify three verbs. However, it would have helped if he had explained the effect of each one even more clearly. He should also have stated what was implied as well as what was stated clearly. One way to do this is to use the **PEA** technique:

- **Point:** One of the linguistic devices that the writer uses is …
- **Evidence:** For example, the writer says …
- **Analysis:** This suggests that … and makes the reader think …

Extract from a Grade 5 answer:

P

> One of the linguistic devices that Mo Farah uses is emotive language. For example, he says that the crowd was 'roaring' him on. The use of the verb roaring is effective because it suggests that the noise in the stadium is unbelievably loud because everyone is supporting the athlete. It also implies that it is a frightening sound as lions usually roar.

E

A

Continue this analysis, exploring some of the other emotive language used in the passage. Use the notes from the table you completed on page 80 to help you.

# 2 Using other linguistic devices to persuade

There are many linguistic devices that writers use in their writing to persuade their readers, including:

- repetition
- listing/lists of three
- personal pronouns
- figurative language
- rhetorical questions
- exaggeration/hyperbole.

## Repetition and lists of three

The extract that follows on page 82 is the 'Gettysburg Address' which was a speech given by the US President Abraham Lincoln on 19 November 1863, during the American Civil War. It is considered one of the most famous speeches in history.

Read the speech carefully. Examples of repetition have been highlighted in red. Examples of lists of three have been highlighted in blue.

Lincoln is referring to the American Declaration of Independence which had been written 87 years previously.

**conceived** means born in

**proposition** means idea

**consecrate** means to make sacred

**hallow** means to make special

Four score and seven years ago our fathers brought forth on this continent a new nation, **conceived** in liberty, and dedicated to the **proposition** that all men are created equal.

Now we are engaged in a great civil war, testing whether that nation, or any nation so conceived and so dedicated, can long endure. We are met on a great battlefield of that war. We have come to dedicate a portion of that field, as a final resting place for those who here gave their lives that that nation might live. It is altogether fitting and proper that we should do this.

But, in a larger sense, we cannot dedicate, we cannot **consecrate**, we cannot **hallow** this ground. The brave men, living and dead, who struggled here, have consecrated it, far above our poor power to add or detract. The world will little note, nor long remember what we say here, but it can never forget what they did here. It is for us the living, rather, to be dedicated here to the unfinished work which they who fought here have thus far so nobly advanced. It is rather for us to be here dedicated to the great task remaining before us—that from these honoured dead we take increased devotion to that cause for which they gave the last full measure of devotion—that we here highly resolve that these dead shall not have died in vain—that this nation, under God, shall have a new birth of freedom—and that government of the people, by the people, for the people, shall not perish from the earth.

Abraham Lincoln, *Gettysburg Address* (1863)

An able student produced a disappointing Grade 3 response about the repetition used. This is an extract:

> Lincoln has repeated the word dedicated on several occasions. This is significant because he is suggesting that, to succeed in war, American citizens must be 'dedicated' or committed to the cause, just like the fallen soldiers who lost their lives. He is using these soldiers to serve as an example to the rest of the American nation, implying to the reader that good American citizens should be like these soldiers.

## ACTIVITY 1

**1** How could this be improved?
**2** Rewrite the above paragraph so that it gets a higher mark. Remember the PEA approach.

In the same response, the student wrote about Lincoln's use of lists of three in the speech.

> Lincoln has also used a list of three when he says 'we cannot dedicate, we cannot consecrate, we cannot hallow.' Here, Lincoln is telling the listener that the land belongs to the American soldiers who 'struggled here, have consecrated it.' Lincoln is implying that the American soldiers will not be forgotten because they will live on in this land.

**3** What should this student have written to gain a higher grade?
**4** Rewrite the paragraph so that it would impress the examiner.

## Personal pronouns

When a writer is writing to persuade, they often use the personal pronoun 'you' to address the reader directly. This is known as direct address. They may also use the personal pronoun 'we' to create the idea that there is agreement.

## ACTIVITY 2

Discussion point

**1** With a friend, discuss why Lincoln used 'we' so many times.
**2** Write a paragraph explaining why you think it has been used and how it is supposed to affect his audience.

## Figurative language

Many writers use figurative language when they are writing to persuade. Figurative language can include similes, metaphors, alliteration and personification.

Read the letter below, which was written in the twentieth century. In it, Beatrice is trying to persuade George to have a relationship with her.

> 18th November 1912
>
> 33 Kensington Square
>
> My dear George,
>
> No more shams -- a real love letter this time -- then I can breathe freely, and perhaps, who knows, begin to sit up and get well --
>
> You must know by now that I adore you. My heart calls to you. I wish that I could kiss you and then you'd know the strength of my feelings. However, I'm a respectable widow so I cannot. I cannot risk society looking at me and judging me.
>
> Oh George I'm so unhappy! I wish you'd take my love seriously. However, when you speak all your words are as idle wind. Just look into my eyes for two minutes and see the love that is trapped within them. Look into my eyes, George, and see what's in my heart.
>
> I long for you, George. Why do you play with my heart? Why do you make excuses? Why don't you care?
>
> Your Beatrice

Beatrice Campbell (20th century)

A student wrote the following about Beatrice's use of language in the letter.

> Beatrice uses the simile 'all your words are as idle wind'. Here she is comparing George's words to the wind. This is a very effective simile.

**Key term**

**Implied:** suggested.

This answer is a Grade 2 standard response. The student was able to identify a simile. However, it would have helped if she had explained the effect of it. She should have stated what was **implied** as well as what was stated clearly.

## ACTIVITY 3

**1** Rewrite the analysis so that it gets more marks.

### Rhetorical questions

Beatrice also uses three rhetorical questions, one after the other, in the letter.

*Why do you play with my heart? Why do you make excuses? Why don't you care?*

## ACTIVITY 4

**1** Explain how Beatrice uses rhetorical questions to convince George that she loves him.

> The use of three rhetorical questions, one after the other, is powerful. It is designed to make George feel … because … Also …

### Hyberbole

**Hyperbole**, is also used by Beatrice to convince George of how much she loves him. In Beatrice's letter, she has used hyperbole when she writes 'then I can breathe freely'.

**Key term**

**Hyperbole:** exaggeration to make a point.

## ACTIVITY 5

**1** What do you think she is hoping the effect will be when George reads 'then I can breathe freely'?

**Boost your grade**

Of course, in the examination you will have to identify different techniques, rather than just dealing with one at a time.

**1** Write a letter to your headteacher or principal, to persuade them to allow a famous artist to perform a concert in your school or academy. Include:
- well-chosen adjectives
- emotive language
- repetition
- listing/lists of three
- personal pronouns
- figurative language
- rhetorical questions
- hyperbole.

**2** Explain to a friend how you have used these features: in each case, what were you hoping the effect would be?

Apply a similar analytical approach to this extract from Winston Churchill's famous 1940 speech, 'We shall fight on the beaches'. Churchill was the British Prime Minister; and Germany seemed to be on the verge of invading the British Isles.

flag means to weaken

subjugated means conquered

I have, myself, full confidence that if all do their duty, if nothing is neglected, and if the best arrangements are made, as they are being made, we shall prove ourselves once again able to defend our Island home, to ride out the storm of war, and to outlive the menace of tyranny, if necessary for years, if necessary alone. At any rate, that is what we are going to try to do. That is the resolve of His Majesty's Government – every man of them. That is the will of Parliament and the nation. The British Empire and the French Republic, linked together in their cause and in their need, will defend to the death their native soil, aiding each other like good comrades to the utmost of their strength. Even though large tracts of Europe and many old and famous States have fallen or may fall into the grip of the Gestapo and all the odious apparatus of Nazi rule, we shall not **flag** or fail. We shall go on to the end, we shall fight in France, we shall fight on the seas and oceans, we shall fight with growing confidence and growing strength in the air, we shall defend our Island, whatever the cost may be, we shall fight on the beaches, we shall fight on the landing grounds, we shall fight in the fields and in the streets, we shall fight in the hills; we shall never surrender, and even if, which I do not for a moment believe, this Island or a large part of it were **subjugated** and starving, then our Empire beyond the seas, armed and guarded by the British Fleet, would carry on the struggle, until, in God's good time, the New World, with all its power and might, steps forth to the rescue and the liberation of the old.

Winston Churchill, 'We shall fight on the beaches' (1940)

**3** List the different techniques he uses and what their effect is intended to be:

| TECHNIQUE | EXAMPLE | EFFECT |
|---|---|---|
| repetition | If all… if nothing… if the best… | |
| personal pronoun | we | |
| | | |

## Test yourself

Read the source opposite, which is an extract from an article from the *Guardian* newspaper. How does Stuart Heritage use language to try to persuade the reader that the challenge is not a good idea?

# How to dodge the ice bucket challenge

*I plan to avoid the fun and retain my dignity*                by Stuart Heritage

- **Ice bucket challenge: who's pouring cold water on the idea?**

- **A celebrity wet T-shirt contest that has nothing to do with charity**

It finally happened. On Saturday afternoon, at two minutes to two – just when I'd begun to convince myself that the whole sorry affair had reached a point of **critical mass** and was about to implode like some sort of unsustainably enormous Red Giant – I was nominated for the **ALS** ice bucket challenge. And I was furious.

Because the ice bucket challenge was supposed to be for celebrities. It was the perfect vehicle for them. It allowed them to show off their palatial homes and brag about all their famous chums and demonstrate how **relatable** and fun and **philanthropic** and just generally better than you they are. It was never meant to be for people like us, the no-mark **schmucks** who could set ourselves on fire and run through a shopping centre screaming our own names without even getting so much as a second glance from anyone. Our lives are crap enough as it is. We shouldn't have to worry about anything as pointless as **gratuitous** shivering as well.

But this weekend, it crossed over. Inspired by the selfless work of their A-list idols, civilians started performing ice bucket challenges

of their own. Facebook immediately transformed into a mess of cousin-in-laws and potentially racist former classmates all hooting and shrieking and failing to realise that you're supposed to hold your phone sideways when you film things. And that was fair enough, I thought, because who'd be silly enough to nominate me? Everyone knows that I'm not the sort of person who'd willingly ever pour water over myself. It might be fun, but I hate fun. I repel fun. I am, largely speaking, the walking manifestation of anti-fun.

And then it happened. My Uncle Vince, driven mad by the act of standing in a pond with a builder's bucket of freezing water in his hands, blurted out my name during his challenge video. He'd apparently meant to nominate my brother Pete – who, by the way, would have

definitely done it, then taken all his clothes off, then Instagrammed himself high-fiving a police officer, then tagged it with the word #Legend 15 times in a row – but it was too late. The damage had been done. I'd been nominated.

That's when it hit me. If the ice bucket challenge is here to stay now – and it is, because things take so long to die on Facebook that I still get poked on a semi-regular basis – then others will find themselves in my position, too. It might be you. You might find yourself being **errantly** nominated for the ice bucket challenge by a misguided acquaintance. You might not know how to react, either. So, in a selfless act of public service, I've decided to show you your options.

Your options are basically a) do it, or b) don't do it.

Stuart Heritage, the *Guardian* (2014)

---

**What you have learned**

**In this unit you have learned to write about:**

- the persuasive techniques used by writers
- similarities and differences between writers' views.

---

**critical mass** means a peak

**ALS** stands for amyotrophic lateral sclerosis – also known as motor neurone disease

**relatable** means in touch (with the public)

**philanthropic** means generous (often for charity)

**schmucks** is a word for fools

**gratuitous** means unnecessary

**errantly** means mistakenly

# Q4 Comparing viewpoints and writers' methods

## What this unit involves

This unit deals with Paper 2, Question 4. You will have to compare writers' ideas and viewpoints, as well as how these are conveyed, across two or more sources.

You will read two passages of non-fiction and answer a question comparing the different ideas that the writers are putting across, and the techniques that the writers have used to show their ideas.

There are 16 marks for this question and you will have 16 or 17 minutes to answer it.

## 1 Comparing viewpoints

When you are comparing sources, you will have to consider the point of view that the writers are trying to convey.

## Practising for success

Read the article below. It is an article about Shah Rukh Khan, a famous Indian actor. Once you have read the article, answer the questions that follow.

**Bollywood superstar Shah Rukh Khan named world's second richest actor**

*Actor, producer and businessman out-earned Tom Cruise in 2013, but was beaten to number one spot by Jerry Seinfeld*

*by Hannah Ellis-Petersen*

Shah Rukh Khan is the only Bollywood star to feature in the top ten of Wealth-X's international rich list for 2013.

Bollywood's highest earning celebrity, Shah Rukh Khan earned in excess of £25m last year, securing his title as the second richest actor in the world.

The 48-year-old Bollywood star, dubbed King Khan, out-earned Hollywood stars such as Tom Cruise and Johnny Depp in 2013, and has an estimated personal fortune of £350m.

Khan has starred in over 50 Hindi films over his glittering 20-year career, co-owns the Indian Premier League cricket team Kolkata Knight Riders, and has his own successful production company. His latest film, Chennai Express, earned him £3m and broke several Bollywood box office records on its debut.

Khan was the only Bollywood star to feature in the top ten of the international celebrity rich list for 2013 – compiled by Wealth-X – and was beaten to the number one spot by Jerry Seinfeld. Married to Indian film producer Gauri Chibber, Khan's vast fortune includes homes in Mumbai, Delhi, Dubai and London.

Bollywood remains the world's largest film-making industry, producing about 1000 films each year – double the output of Hollywood.

Hannah Ellis-Petersen, the *Guardian* (2014)

## ACTIVITY 1

Discussion point

**1** What is the writer's attitude towards Shah Rukh Khan? How can you tell?

This is the opening to a student response.

> The writer feels that Shah Rukh Khan is very successful. We can tell this because he uses lots of facts to suggest this. For example, he writes that 'his latest film, Chennai Express, earned him £3m and broke several Bollywood box office records on its debut.' This suggests that Shah Rukh Khan earns a lot of money and makes good films.

Assessment comment

This answer was Grade 4 standard. Although the student has used a quotation and supported their idea here, they needed to talk about the effect of the language in more detail. They also need to consider what is implied as well as what is stated clearly. Finally, the student refers to the writer as 'he'. However, if you read the article carefully you will realise that the writer is actually a woman!

**2** Rewrite the paragraph so that it gets a higher mark. If you are stuck, use the following paragraph structure to help you:

> The writer feels...
>
> We know this because...
>
> This suggests...
>
> This also implies that...

**3** The writer has used several noun phrases to exemplify Khan's success. Copy and complete the table below, analysing the effect of these phrases. The first one has been done for you:

**Key term**

**Noun phrase**: a noun is the name of a person, place or thing; a noun phrase is a phrase playing the role of a man.

| PHRASE | WHAT THIS SUGGESTS |
|---|---|
| *world's second richest actor* | The phrase 'second richest actor' suggests that he is extremely wealthy.<br><br>This implies that he is very successful. However, 'second richest' shows that there is another actor in the world who is even wealthier than he is. |
| *glittering 20-year career* | |
| *successful production company* | |
| *vast fortune* | |

Now read the article below. It is an article about the death of Marilyn Monroe in 1962.

**Marilyn Monroe found dead**

Film star Marilyn Monroe has been found dead in her home in Los Angeles. She was just 36 years of age.

The screen icon's body was discovered this morning. A concerned housekeeper called medical staff when she failed to wake her employer.

She was found lying in her bed with an empty bottle of tablets believed to be sleeping pills by her side.

Many believe that Monroe's death indicated a "possible suicide".

Millions of fans around the world are completely distraught by the star's premature and tragic death.

**4** What is the writer's attitude towards Marilyn Monroe in this article?

**5** Copy and fill in the table below, considering some of the noun phrases used in this article. The first one has been done for you.

| PHRASE | WHAT THIS IMPLIES |
|---|---|
| The screen icon | The phrase *'screen icon'* suggests that she is an extremely famous actress.<br><br>The word *'icon'* also suggests that people adored her, or even worshipped her. |
| just 36 years of age | |
| concerned housekeeper | |
| possible suicide | |
| completely distraught | |
| premature and tragic death | |

**6** How is the tone of this article different to the tone in the article about Shah Rukh Khan? See page 75 for how to compare.

A student wrote the following paragraph comparing the writer's attitude in this article to the writer's attitude in the *Guardian* article.

Both of the articles are about film stars. The first is about an Indian film star and the second is about an American film star. The second article is sadder than the first article because the film star is dead. In the first article we learn a lot about how much money the film star has but in the second article we don't.

This paragraph is Grade 3 standard. Although there is a comparison, comments are not developed and there is no evidence.

Another student wrote the following paragraph:

In the *Guardian* article the writer feels very positive about Shah Rukh Khan. We can tell this because she refers to his 'glittering 20-year career'. The adjective 'glittering' here suggests that his career has been very successful. By using the adjective the writer is also implying that he is a superstar and that people have noticed his films. In the second article the writer is also very positive about Marilyn Monroe. The writer refers to her as a 'screen icon'. This suggests that she has been a big superstar on the Hollywood screen. The phrase 'icon' also implies that she is adored and almost worshipped by her fans.

Assessment comment

This paragraph is Grade 5 standard. The student has made detailed references to the attitudes of both writers. They have also used evidence to back up the points that they have made. Also, the student has considered what is implied as well as what is stated clearly. By 'zooming in' on the two phrases they are able to write about them in much more detail.

**7** Now write two more paragraphs comparing both of the articles. Use the tables that you did on pages 90 and 91 to help you.

## 2 Comparing methods

When you are comparing sources, you will not only comment on the point of view that the writers are trying to convey, you will also have to write about the different methods that they use. Writers use many different methods to engage their readers. These techniques could include using:

- interesting verbs and adverbs
- interesting nouns and adjectives
- listing/lists of three
- juxtaposition and contrast
- other linguistic techniques such as rhetorical questions, emotive language, figurative language or hyperbole
- anecdote or humour.

# Practising for success

Read the following extract. It is taken from a book called *Manners for Women* by Mrs Humphry, which was first published in 1897. Once you have read the extract, answer the questions that follow.

One can almost invariably distinguish the well-bred girl at the first glance, whether she is walking, shopping, in an **omnibus**, descending from a carriage or a cab, or sauntering up and down in the park. Though the fashionable manner inclines to a rather marked decisiveness and the fashionable voice to loudness, even harshness, there is a quiet self-possession about the gentlewoman, whether young or old, that marks her out from women of a lower class, whose manner is **florid**. This is perhaps the best word to describe the lively gestures, the notice-attracting glance and the self-conscious air of the **underbred**, who continually appear to wish to impress their personality upon all they meet.

**Self-effacement** is as much the rule of good manners in the street as it is in society. The well-bred woman goes quietly along, intent on her own business and regardless of the rest of the world, except in so far as to keep from intruding upon their personal rights.

Mrs Humphry, *Manners for Women* (1897)

**omnibus** is a bus or tram

**florid** means showy

**underbred** are people who the writer considers don't have manners

**self-effacement** means modesty

## ACTIVITY 1

1 How does Mrs Humphry, the author, think that women should behave in public?

2 What sort of writing does the extract appear to be? How can you tell?

Now you are going to attempt to analyse the language used in the extract.

3 Read the extract again carefully. Can you find any of the following which give you an idea about how, according to Mrs Humphry, women are expected to behave:

- interesting verbs and adverbs
- interesting adjectives
- use of listing
- use of juxtaposition/contrast?

4 Now copy and complete the table on page 94 analysing how language is used to show how women in society at the time were expected to behave.

| LINGUISTIC FEATURE | EXAMPLE | WHAT IS SUGGESTED/IMPLIED |
| --- | --- | --- |
| Interesting verbs and adverbs | **'goes quietly** along' | This suggests that women should keep themselves to themselves and that women of a higher class should not make their voices heard. |
| Interesting adjectives | **'well-bred** girl' | |
| Use of listing | '…walking, shopping, in an omnibus, descending from a carriage or a cab, or sauntering up and down in the park.' | |
| Use of juxtaposition/ contrast | '…that marks her out from women of a lower class, whose manner is florid.' | |

Discussion point

**5** Now read the article below, which is from the *Daily Telegraph*. How does the writer of this article feel that women need to behave at work? What differences can you find between this article and Mrs Humphry's self-help book?

**alpha male** is a dominant and masculine male

**Women feel need to 'act like men' to get ahead at work**

By Louisa Peacock, Deputy Women's Editor

Many women are conforming to outdated stereotypes and acting "like an **alpha male**" to succeed at work — including dressing like a man, hiding 'girlie' emotions and being outspoken, new research shows.

One in four women dress in a more masculine way — discarding high heels and dresses for trouser suits — acting under the belief they should look like their male colleagues to be treated seriously. A further quarter wear less make-up at work, the survey of 2,000 working women showed.

Half hide their true emotions — with two fifths admitting to having left the office to cry — while a fifth believe they need to act ruthlessly to be respected at work. A small number, one in 20, actively mirror the behaviour of male colleagues

The research, by telecommunications firm O2, suggested the lack of female role models at the top of business was partly to blame for why so many women felt the need to look or act like their male colleagues to succeed.

Louisa Peacock, *The Telegraph* (2013)

**6** Now copy and complete the table below, considering the similarities and differences between this extract and Mrs Humphry's self-help book.

| | MRS HUMPHRY | TELEGRAPH ARTICLE |
|---|---|---|
| The way women are presented | Mrs Humphry suggests that well-bred women should stay in the background. | The writer says that women who want to be more successful at work have had to start acting like men. |
| The tone of the article | Mrs Humphry is quite authoritative and assertive in tone. We do not hear from any women except the author. | The writer has a neutral tone, reporting the situation. |
| Interesting verbs and adverbs | | |
| Interesting adjectives | | |
| Use of juxtaposition/contrast | | |

A student wrote the following paragraph, comparing how women are presented in both extracts.

> In the first extract the writer thinks that women should stay quiet and know their place. However, in the second extract the writer feels that women have to act like men in the workplace if they wish to succeed. The writer of the second source is more sympathetic towards women than the writer of the first source.

**7** Rewrite the paragraph so that it gets a higher grade. Use the following paragraph structure to help you:

> In Source A, the writer feels...
>
> This is evident when they say...
>
> This suggests...
>
> It also implies...
>
> However, in Source B the writer feels...
>
> This is evident when they say...
>
> This suggests...
>
> It also implies that...

**Assessment comment**

So far this response only achieved a Grade 3. Although the student has made a direct comparison they haven't developed this comparison or used quotations.

**8** Now choose an interesting linguistic technique that both writers have used (use the table that you filled in on page 91 to help you). Write a second paragraph comparing the way both writers have used the linguistic technique. Use the following paragraph structure to help you:

In Source A, the writer has used...

This is evident when they say...

This suggests...

It also implies...

In Source B the writer has also used...

This is evident when they say...

This suggests...

It also implies that...

## 3 Developing comparisons

For Question 4 of the exam, you are required to compare two sources, looking at the attitudes of the writers and methods used by the writers to explore these attitudes. Remind yourself of how to compare sources (p.75).

## Practising for success

Read the two sources that follow. The first is the **obituary** of Alexander Graham Bell, the inventor of the telephone, which was published in the *New York Times*. The second is an extract from a biography about him.

> **Key term**
>
> **Obituary:** A notice of death often found in a newspaper.

> **anaemia** is an illness that decreases the amount of red blood cells that a person has

**Source A**

**August 3, 1922**

**OBITUARY**

**Dr. Bell, Inventor of Telephone, Dies**

*By THE NEW YORK TIMES*

SYDNEY, N. S., Aug. 2.--Dr. Alexander Graham Bell, inventor of the telephone, died at 2 o'clock this morning at Beinn Breagh, his estate near Baddeck.

Although the inventor, who was in his seventy-sixth year, had been in failing health for several months, he had not been confined to bed, and the end was unexpected. Late yesterday afternoon, however, his condition, brought about by progressive **anaemia**, became serious, and Dr. Ker of Washington, a cousin of Mrs. Bell, a house guest and a Sydney physician, attended him.

With Mr. Bell when he died were Mrs. Bell, a daughter, Mrs. Marion Hubbard Fairchild, and her husband, David G. Fairchild of Washington. The inventor leaves another daughter, Mrs. Elise M. Grosvenor, wife of Gilbert Grosvenor of Washington, who now is with her husband in Brazil.

Dr. Bell asked to be buried in the countryside where he had spent the major portion of the last thirty-five years of his life. The inventor came to Cape Breton forty years ago, and five years later purchased the Beinn Breagh estate. His last experiments, dealing with flying boats, were made on Bras d'Or Lake.

American specialists who were rushing to the bedside of Dr. Bell were today returning to the United States. They were told of his death while aboard fast trains bound for Baddeck, and, being too late, turned back.

*New York Times* (1922)

## Source B
### Alexander Graham Bell Biography

*Educator, Linguist, Inventor, Scientist (1847–1922)*

Alexander Graham Bell was one of the primary inventors of the telephone, did important work in communication for the deaf and held more than 18 patents.

*Final Years*

In the last 30 years of his life, Bell was involved in a wide range of projects and pursued them at a furious pace. He worked on inventions in flight (the tetrahedral kite), scientific publications (Science magazine), and exploration of the earth (National Geographic magazine).

Alexander Graham Bell died peacefully, with his wife by his side, in Cape Breton Island, Nova Scotia, Canada, on August 2, 1922. The entire telephone system was shut down for one minute in tribute to his life. Within a few months, his wife also passed away. Alexander Graham Bell's contribution to the modern world and its technologies was enormous.

www.biography.com

## ACTIVITY 1

Question: Compare how the two writers convey their different attitudes to the death of Alexander Graham Bell.

In your answer, you should:
- compare their different attitudes
- compare the methods they use to convey their attitudes
- support your ideas with quotations from both sources.

1 Read the question and sources carefully.

2 Draw a table or write a paragraph plan, considering the similarities and differences between the sources and the writers' attitudes and methods. Copy and complete the table on page 98.

**Examiner comment**

In the exam, you might not have time to write a detailed plan. Instead, you can highlight the sources themselves and add quick annotations.

| POINT | EVIDENCE | WHAT EVIDENCE SUGGESTS/ IMPLIES |
|---|---|---|
| Source A – Attitude of writer towards death | | |
| Source B – Attitude of writer towards death | | |
| Source A – A method the writer uses | | |
| Source B – A method the writer uses | | |
| Source A – Another method the writer uses | | |
| Source B – Another method the writer uses | | |

3 Write your answer. Make sure you include the following in each paragraph:

- a clear opening statement that is linked to the question
- evidence from the source
- what the evidence suggests
- what is implied.

4 Make sure that you compare throughout. You can do this by using connectives such as 'in contrast', 'however' and 'whereas'.

5 Make sure that you have a conclusion where you summarise the similarities and differences between the sources, as well as the different methods that the writers have used.
e.g. Overall, therefore, there are similarities between the attitudes to Alexander Graham Bell's death… However there are also differences because… Their methods are different too…

## Test yourself

For this question, you need to refer to the whole of **Source A**, an article from the *Daily Telegraph* newspaper about World War I, together with **Source B**, a letter from a soldier, George Clarke, who died in the **Boer War**.

Compare how the two writers convey their different attitudes to war.

In your answer, you should:

- compare their different attitudes
- compare the methods they use to convey their attitudes
- support your ideas with quotations from both sources.

The **Boer War** was fought between the British Empire and South African forces known as the Boers between 1899 and 1902.

**Source A**

# Remembering sacrifices of the past – and present

*The coming centenary of the First World War should bring attention to the remarkable actions that the Services perform for their countrymen*

When it is said of war, "never forget", that surely means we should remember the sacrifices of the present as well as those of the past. Although, as the centenary of the outbreak of the First World War approaches, people's minds inevitably return to history.

Reading the front pages of The Daily Telegraph 100 years ago, it is striking how similar pre-war society was to contemporary Britain. Overseas, of course, there were reports of a gathering crisis in Vienna: the Archduke had been assassinated by a Serbian nationalist, Russian and German diplomats were on manoeuvres, and Britain looked on with a mix of apprehension and confusion.

But the newspaper also carried all the hallmarks of "business as usual". Wimbledon and Henley were finished, the summer sales were on. People could purchase a new dress, a place at a music school for gentlewomen, shares in Marconi's Wireless Telegraph Company, or even a cruise to German East Africa. It was far from obvious that on July 28 Vienna would declare war on Serbia, and that by August 4

Britain would be at war with Germany. By the time the Armistice was signed in 1918, hundreds of thousands of British soldiers would be dead – many lost to the horrors of the Western front. The centenary is an opportunity to pay respect to those men, to ensure that the memory of their sacrifice is passed down to future generations.

Of course, at the heart of our security is the soldier; the man or woman prepared to lay down their life for their fellow countrymen. Yesterday witnessed the celebration of three such heroes when they received the Military Cross at Buckingham Palace: Cpl William Mills of 4th Battalion, The Rifles; Major

Geoffrey Brocklehurst, of the Royal Regiment of Scotland; and WO1 Patrick Hyde, Regimental Sgt Major of the 4th Battalion, The Rifles.

WO1 Hyde was dubbed the "bomb magnet" after being blown up 17 times in Afghanistan and Iraq, which he unflappably called "an occupational hazard". He was being recognised at the Palace for an incident in which he continued to organise the rescue of his comrades despite having been injured himself. He said: "I remember it bloody hurt. I thought I had lost my leg, but fortunately it was still there and once the dust had settled, we got out of there." Those are the cool, calm tones of the ideal British soldier.

*The Telegraph* (2014)

**Source B**

*Frere, Wednesday*

*I have so little time in Camp and that I spend in eating and sleeping, that I must continue this letter on odd bits of paper at odd moments during the day. On Saturday night we heard that the Boers were retiring to Colenso, and on Sunday morning at 5 am we were ordered to leave Estcourt, and by 8 am, had left for Frere Station. Although the march was only 12 miles we did not reach Frere until 4 pm. We then had to go to the hills to watch for the Boers and we did not get to the camping ground till dark. Our baggage never arrived that night and we lay out in the open. We had no breakfast before starting but got some bully beef and biscuits in the evening.*

*The Boers had just left Frere station before we arrived, and had blown up a big railway bridge, and ransacked all the houses. I have never seen such a state as they left the houses in. They even cut open the mattresses in hopes of finding money hidden there. Nothing of any value was left except a cat and some dogs, which have joined our army. The remains of the armoured train which the Boers destroyed are near here. I wish I had a camera with me. On Monday morning we had to go out on **picquet** and the guns were left out on the hills all day. In the afternoon we fired at a party of 50 Boers at a range of 4,800 yards, but only frightened them. They were too far off to do any damage. On Tuesday morning one section went on outpost duty, the remainder of the Battery went out on a reconnaissance. Unfortunately I had taken some poison and was very bad in the morning, and so was selected for the officer to stay behind in Camp.*

*They had a very good day, lots of firing – and plenty of the enemy's shell fell into the Battery without however doing any damage. I expect our shooting was more effective. The Boers have very good guns and they shoot very accurately but their shell don't burst properly, and unless the shell happens to strike a man it does no damage.*

> **piquet** – soldiers placed in a forward position in preparation of an enemy advance.

They did not succeed in hitting any of the Cavalry either. One of the guns was upset going over an ant heap and a gunner's leg was crushed. Today we are out again on the hill on outpost duty. It is very slow work, especially today as the Boers have blown up Colenso Bridge, and must have cleared out of this part altogether. I don't expect we will leave this place until the railway bridge is mended. The 68th Battery has joined us. The line is open again from here to Durban... The Boers have left a good deal of cattle and some sheep which they have looted. We have now got large herds in the Camp. They are very fine beasts much better than anything Charlie can boast of. I have seen some draught oxen standing 17 hands high... This is a great place for insects, but there are no mosquitoes or any animals that annoy one. There are very fine beetles, butterflies and grasshoppers... We hear firing going on at Ladysmith every day and are now about 25 miles from there. The Boers have got a very strong position at Colenso, and the river Tugela, which is too deep to ford, flows between us and them. I expect we will have a rough time turning them out. I think this is a very healthy place, I have never felt tired and seldom hungry, and except on two occasions I have been very well...

Marshal George Clarke

## What you have learned

**In this unit you have learned how to write about:**

- the different attitudes of writers
- the tone of the sources and how they are similar or different
- writers' methods
- sources and how to compare them.

# Papers 1 and 2, Section B

## What you have to do...

On both papers, you should have spent approximately 60 minutes on Section A, which leaves you 45 minutes for Section B. You will have to write one essay for each paper.

## How to divide up your time

If you are wise, you will spend:
- 4 or 5 minutes planning
- 35 minutes writing
- 5 minutes checking and improving your work.

## What you will have to write

### Paper 1

Paper 1 will give you a choice of two questions and you must choose to answer just one of them. You will get:
- two questions asking you to describe
  **or**
- two questions asking you to produce a piece of narrative writing (story)
  **or**
- two questions offering you different forms of writing: one question asking you to produce a piece of description and one asking you to write a narrative.

### Paper 2

You will have no choice of questions on Paper 2.

You will have to answer the one question offered, which will ask for your point of view on some issue.

The marks will be awarded in the same way for both papers.

| 24 MARKS | For content and organisation | Ideas, ability to deal with purpose and audience, use of language, structure and paragraphing |
|---|---|---|
| 16 MARKS | For technical accuracy | Sentences, punctuation, spelling, vocabulary and use of Standard English |

# Communicating effectively

In this unit you will learn how to adapt your language to:
⇨ appeal to different audiences
⇨ fulfil different purposes.

## 1 Adapting your language for specific audiences

All texts are written with an audience in mind. Writers make specific choices about the language they will use depending on the audience they are writing for. When you produce a piece of writing, you need to think carefully about who the audience is and how you will use language to interest them.

## Practising for success

Read through the following extracts.

### Source A

> Sophie opened the door, and there was a big, furry, stripy tiger. The tiger said, 'Excuse me, but I'm very hungry. Do you think I could have tea with you?' Sophie's mummy said, 'Of course, come in.'

Judith Kerr, *The Tiger Who Came To Tea* (1968)

### Source B

> It's new issue day and we've brought you a fabulous summer edition for you to get your grubby little mitts on. Here's why you need it in your life:
>
> One Direction – are on the cover. We've got the low down on their life in the limelight, their firm friendship and why they haven't changed one tiny bit…

TOTP Mag (2014)

## Source C

> *Dear Mr Jones*
>
> *I am writing to complain about the refuse collection in my neighbourhood recently. Since June, the days and time of the refuse collection have varied considerably each week — and some weeks, the bins have not been emptied at all. This is a disgrace! Especially in the summer months, the streets become smelly as the roads are lined with overflowing wheelie bins. I demand to know what you are going to do about this.*

### ACTIVITY 1

**1 a)** Who do you think is the audience for each source?

   **b)** Explain how you think the language in each extract appeals to this audience. Try to find an example to support your point.

**2 a)** What do you notice about the **formality** of each source?

- Find a word or phrase from each source to support your point.
- Where would you place each source on this scale?

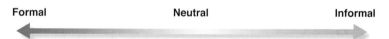

| Formal | Neutral | Informal |

   **b)** Explain why you think it is important to think about formality when you are writing for a specific audience.

**3** What approach has each writer taken towards the reader? Copy and complete the table below.

Decide on:

- the **tone** of the source
- the way the writer wants the reader to feel or react.

Then:

- find a word or phrase from each extract to support your point.

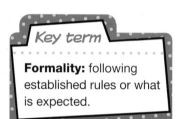

**Key term**

**Formality:** following established rules or what is expected.

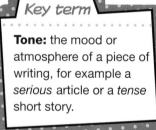

**Key term**

**Tone:** the mood or atmosphere of a piece of writing, for example a *serious* article or a *tense* short story.

| SOURCE | TONE | HOW WE SHOULD FEEL | KIND OF LANGUAGE USED |
|---|---|---|---|
| A | | | |
| B | | | |
| C | | | |

This student has written an opening to a speech for the parents of the new Year 7 students at her school.

> Alright guys? So, you must be getting dead worried right about your little kids starting big school after the hols. Don't stress though. As long as you've got all the stuff sorted everything'll be cool ok? What you don't want is your kid coming to school and being like 'Mum, you forgot my pencil case' or something like that. That'd be rubbish!

**4 a)** Rewrite the passage to make it more appropriate for this audience. Think carefully about the words and formality you will use and the approach you want to take towards the audience.

**b)** Explain the changes that you made and why. Think about:

- the impression you wanted to give of yourself as a writer
- the way you wanted your audience to react and feel.

**5** Read this example exam writing task and notice the highlighted key words.

> Sport should be compulsory for all students in school up to the age of 16. Students should have a PE lesson twice a week and should be encouraged to join a school sports team.

Key words in the task tell you the topic that you will have to write about.

The task also makes clear the format of the writing.

**Write an** entry for a school magazine **in which you** explain your viewpoint **on this issue.**

Other key words tell you the purpose of your writing.

**6** Now think specifically about how the topic and audience will influence the language choices you make. Create a list of at least six features of language you are going to include, e.g.:

- lots of words to do with sport and health
- engaging **pronouns** (e.g. you, we, I)
- **emotive language** to win over the readers (e.g. surely you would like to be fitter …).

**7** Now write your opening paragraph in response to this task.

---

**Examiner comment**

It is vital to keep the audience in mind. In the exam, you will always be writing formally, so avoid slang or **colloquialisms**.

**Key term**

**Colloquialism:** informal use of language.

**Key terms**

**Pronouns:** replace nouns (e.g. you, we, I).

**Emotive language:** produces a strong emotional response in the reader.

**Read this student's opening paragraph to the school magazine entry about sport in schools.**

**How well has this student engaged his audience of students, parents and teachers?**

Good use of vocabulary

Rhetorical question to engage

> Obesity. It seems that everywhere you look there is an article or news story about it, isn't there? There's a good reason for this. Recently, there has been a huge rise in obesity in the UK and the majority of this applies to young people like us who are aged 8–16. It is for this reason that I feel sport should be absolutely compulsory for all students in secondary school. Through participating regularly in sports, we teenagers will become fitter, more energetic and less obese. That can only be a good thing.

Clear viewpoint

Sentences well-controlled, though all relatively unambitious

List of three

For communicating to an audience, this student is heading for a Grade 5 because:
- the communication is clear and convincing
- the tone, style and level of formality is matched to audience.

Look back at your opening paragraph. Rewrite it if you did not have a clear viewpoint or at least two linguistic techniques.

## 2 Adapting your language for specific purposes

All sources are written with a clear purpose in mind. Here you will focus on understanding the difference between sources that are written to describe, narrate and express a viewpoint, because those are the styles of writing you will encounter in the exam.

## Practising for success

Read the following extracts.

### Source A

> The once bland and boring landscape was now alive with colour and light. There were people of all ages as far as the eye could see: some were talking excitedly, some were singing and dancing, others were relaxing in the bright summer sunshine. Smells of delicious food and drink hung over them and a steady beat of drums and guitars drifted on the wind. The festival had come to town.

## Source B

> And the thing I hate most about school is all the homework we get. It's not enough that we have to sit through class after class and try to stay awake while they fill our heads with all this stuff we will probably never need to know, like how to figure out the surface area of a cube or what the difference is between kinetic and potential energy. I'm like, who cares? I've never, ever heard my parents say the word 'kinetic' in my entire life!
>
> R J Palacio, *Wonder* (2012)

## Source C

> Ashley stopped at the traffic lights on the Row, looked across the road – and saw the best wall in the world.
>
> And it had been there all her life.
>
> Jabbing her elbow into Vikki's ribs, she rasied her eyebrows and nodded over the road, towards Fat Annie's and the chippie. Vikki followed where she was looking, and her eyebrows almost disappeared into her hair.
>
> 'Ash! You can't!'
>
> Gillian Cross, *Tightrope* (1999)

## ACTIVITY 1

**1 a)** What is the purpose of each extract?

**b)** Comment on some specific language features in each extract that help the source to achieve its purpose. Use examples to support the points you make.

| SOURCE | PURPOSE | LANGUAGE FEATURES | TONE |
|--------|---------|-------------------|------|
| A | | | |
| B | | | |
| C | | | |

**c)** Comment on the tone of each extract.

- What atmosphere or mood is created in each one?

- How does each extract make the reader feel or react?

- How has language helped to achieve this tone?

## Writing to describe

To achieve your purpose of describing, you will need to use lots of descriptive techniques such as adjectives, verbs, adverbs, the senses, similes and metaphors.

### ACTIVITY 2

**1 a)** Which descriptive techniques can you find in this passage? List them.

> The moon shone down brightly like the bright beam from a flashlight. It lit up the sea below as it splashed gently against the shore. There was no sound other than the soft swooshing of the waves. The night air was cool and calm.

**b)** Notice the peaceful and relaxing tone of this description. Which words or phrases help to create this atmosphere?

**c)** How would a beach be different in daytime? How would the atmosphere change? Write your own short description of a beach in daytime.

## Writing to narrate

When you write a short story you will still use lots of the elements of description. However, you will also need to think about plot, setting and character.

### ACTIVITY 3

Read the following extract on page 109 from *The Bunker Diary* by Kevin Brooks. In it, the narrator sees a character called Bird get attacked by a dog, and another character Fred tries to help.

...No growling, no barking, nothing — just a black streak, and a flash of wicked teeth. It was breathtaking. Bird twisted away and threw his hands up to protect his throat, but the dog was on him like a guided missile. It jumped up and sank its teeth into his neck, just above the shoulder, and Bird screamed and fell to the floor with the dog on top of him.

I couldn't move. I was petrified. But Fred was already up and running. Before I knew what was happening he was halfway down the corridor, whipping the belt from his trousers as he ran, heading for Bird and the dog. Bird was sobbing now, a terrible, gut-wrenching sound...

Kevin Brooks, *The Bunker Diary* (2013)

**1 a)** Narratives focus on characters, events and settings. What can you find out about 'who, what and where' from this extract?

**b)** What do you notice about the language that the writer has used to bring the story to life?

**c)** What atmosphere is created here? How does the extract make the reader feel or react? Which words or phrases help to create this atmosphere?

**d)** Write the next two paragraphs of this story. You might continue with the same tone or atmosphere or change it to make it more positive and calm. What language choices will you make to create an atmosphere, and engage your reader?

Remember to think about your language choices, and to continue to tell the reader about characters, settings and events.

**Examiner comment**

Notice how atmosphere is created in the stories you read at school and at home. That knowledge will feed into your own writing.

## Writing to express a viewpoint

When you write to express a viewpoint your purpose is to give your opinion about something. However, you should also try to engage the reader and persuade them to your point of view.

### ACTIVITY 4

Read this extract from a TV review:

The digital station FX punches above its weight in terms of top-notch TV series. The Wire, Generation Kill, Dexter, Breaking Bad. All of them received their first showing over here on Sky channel 164. Well now it's got The Listener to add to that list. Just to bring down the average.

The Listener isn't a very good example of a high-quality American import. Mainly because it's Canadian, but more importantly because it's rubbish. In fact, even the title is rubbish. You know why it's called The Listener? Because the main character listens to things.

OK, so they're not common-or-garden things. He listens to people's thoughts. He's telepathic... That's actually a fairly interesting premise, so why pick the most boring title imaginable? It's like creating a Superman series and calling it The Flyer.

Charlie Brooker, *The Hell of it All* (2009)

1 Find an example of:
- opinion
- evidence/examples to support the opinion.

2 How might these techniques persuade a reader to agree with Brooker's viewpoint?

3 Find an example of the following techniques. Again consider how they help to convey the writer's viewpoint and persuade a reader to agree:
- humour
- questions
- repetition.

Discussion point

4 What is the tone of this extract? How does the extract make the reader think or feel? How has language been used to create this tone?

5 Write a review of a TV show you have watched. Express your viewpoint about this programme and try to persuade your readers to agree with you.

Boost your grade

Read this extract from a student's description of a beach, which would receive a Grade 5.

What language has she used to create the scene and how? What tone or atmosphere has she created and how?

> At first it seemed quiet. All I could hear was the squawk of a group of seagulls flying in circles in the distance. As I rounded the corner however, the beat of music filled my ears. As I got closer to the beach, the beat turned to music – dance music. I could now see it. The beach was swarming with people running, playing, dancing or just relaxing in the hot sun. It was packed!

Can you improve this writing still further? Rewrite it, and try to:
- use one or two longer sentences
- include a rhetorical question
- add a simile or metaphor
- add some alliteration.

## Test yourself

Write the opening sections of these three exam tasks, demonstrating that you clearly understand the audience and purpose for each of them.

**Paper 1 tasks:**

You are going to enter a creative writing competition.

Your entry will be judged by people your own age.

Either:

Write a description of a beach in winter.

Or:

Write the opening part of a story that begins 'The wind howled.'

**Paper 2 task:**

You see this poster on a school bulletin board:

Write a letter to your headteacher, giving your viewpoint on this subject, outlining what you think should be done about it and why.

> • Have you ever noticed how much paper gets thrown away in each classroom every day?
> • Have you seen how much food in the canteen is wasted each week?
> • Do you know that over 70% of students and staff travel to school in a car, rather than on public transport or a bike?
>
> This has got to stop! Join our campaign. Write a letter to the head teacher telling her what you think about the environmentally un-friendly nature of our school. Together we <u>CAN</u> beat it.

### What you have learned

**In this unit you have learned how:**

- language and tone can be adapted for different audiences and purposes
- to make choices for your own writing to make sure it is well matched to purpose and audience.

# Organising your writing

**What this unit involves**

Your writing responses need to be well-organised because you need to ensure your responses make good sense to the reader.

You are assessed on your ability to organise your ideas.

**In this unit you will learn how to:**
⇒ plan an extended piece of writing
⇒ use **connectives** to make links between and within paragraphs.

### Key term

**Connectives:** words or phrases which link and sequence ideas in sentences, paragraphs and whole texts.

## 1 How to plan

Planning is essential for any writing task you have to do. You need a planning system to help you get all the ideas that are in your head down on to paper and then organise them in a way that will make sense to a reader.

## Practising for success

### ACTIVITY 1

Read the following writing task.

You see this competition in your favourite magazine:

Have you ever had a job experience that didn't go according to plan? We'd love to hear about it!

Write a short story telling us about it and win the chance to have it published in next month's issue!

job experience

**1** Rather than just starting to write, you should always devise a plan first. You need a technique that you follow every time.

This is a four-stage planning technique:
- Underline all the key words in the task so you are focused on the following questions. What is the topic? What is the purpose? Who is the audience?
- Produce a spider diagram of ideas. Write down all your ideas about this experience, for example:

**Examiner comment**

You can use this approach for the writing sections of both English papers, but also in other school subjects. It is often the key to improved performance in essay writing.

- Begin to list these ideas in the order in which you want to write about them. Which ideas can be grouped together in a paragraph? Give each paragraph a topic heading. Leave a space under each heading.
- Now, fill in the gaps, indicating what, exactly, will go in that section or paragraph (particular information, a simile, a quotation, an **anecdote** … or whatever).

**Key term**

**Anecdote:** a short, sometimes entertaining story from personal experience.

**2** Consider this plan:

Getting my first weekend job

**Paragraph 1.**
**Reasons why**
- Saving for an iPhone
- Mum's idea
- Old enough now
- Like doing friend's hair
- Possible career option

**Paragraph 2.**
**Arriving at the salon**
- 10am Saturday
- Already busy
- Hot, humid and smelly
- Hair all over the floor

**Paragraph 3.**
**The boss**

**Examiner comment**

In the exam, you need to be able to produce your plan in four minutes (five minutes maximum!). As with anything else, practice makes perfect: the more essay plans you produce, the quicker it all becomes.

**3** Try this approach yourself. Produce your own plan in response to the task. (On this occasion, if you have never had a job, just make it up!)

## Organisation within paragraphs

It is essential to start each paragraph effectively.

Read this extract. It is taken from an article in the *Sunday Times* newspaper. In it, ex-footballer David Beckham tells us about his typical day. Victoria is his wife and Brooklyn and Harper are the names of two of his children.

I'm usually up early and will spend about five minutes getting ready. Once I've been in the shower, I'll put on deodorant, aftershave and moisturiser, and style my hair. I then get the kids up around 7.30, but getting the four of them ready can be a bit more of a challenge.

If I'm at home for the day, which I often am, I'll also do the kids' breakfast. It's healthy food, but if one of them wants a pancake with a bit of syrup, I'll give it to them.

I then take the kids to school and, thankfully, we don't get pestered by the paparazzi any more. The only one we don't walk to the door is Brooklyn. Sometimes, he makes me drop him on the other side of the road. It's not cool to be dropped off by your dad.

When you have kids, structure can go out the window, but though I've retired from football, I still have a lot going on. Some of it is brand-related. One of my projects is being an Active Kids ambassador for Sainsbury's, so the other day I was shooting a TV ad for them. It's to inspire kids to be healthy, to be active, and I enjoy it.

Generally, I don't have a problem moving around London. I get in the car, or on my bike, and I usually wear a cap and a coat, and just keep my head down. Sometimes I get spotted in a shop and get mobbed, but if I'm quick I can be in and out without being noticed by anyone. I also do the weekly food shop — in fact, I've always done it. People are surprised about that, but it's easy; I know exactly what the kids like and I know exactly what Victoria likes.

Once Harper's home for lunch, I'll make her something to eat. One of her favourite vegetables is broccoli — she calls them trees.

Mark Edmonds, *Sunday Times Magazine* (2014)

## ACTIVITY 2

1 Look carefully at the **topic sentence** in each paragraph. Then notice how the rest of the paragraph adds to this topic. Use this information to sum up in one sentence what each paragraph is about. Record your notes in a table.

2 Copy and complete the table below by recording the connectives that have been used to link the paragraphs. Explain how each one helps to link ideas and guide the reader.

**Key term**

**Topic sentence:** the first sentence in a paragraph, which expresses the main focus or idea of the paragraph.

| PARAGRAPH NUMBER | WHAT IT'S ABOUT | CONNECTIVE USED. HOW THESE GUIDE THE READER |
|---|---|---|
| 1 | He is talking about what he does to get ready in the mornings. | |
| 2 | He tells us what he does on a day when he is at home. | 'If' gives one scenario, then another 'if' develops the idea. |
| | | |

You can use a range of connectives to make different sorts of links between your own paragraphs.

In narrative or descriptive writing you will often link paragraphs by time or place. For example:
- time – suddenly, later that day, the next morning …
- place – over in the distance …

When you are writing to express a viewpoint you will use a range of different connectives for adding to, comparing and contrasting your points. For example:
- adding – in addition, furthermore …
- comparing – similarly …
- contrasting – on the other hand …

3 What other examples can you think of?

## Paragraph lengths

## ACTIVITY 3

1 You can also use a range of paragraph lengths in your writing to create different effects.

Read the extract that follows on page 116. In it Chas and his friend Devil steal a lorry.

I keep thinking I see blue flashing lights on the horizon. Ok, here's the turning. We bomb up the slip road so fast, even Devil grips the side of his seat. We slide round the roundabout and tank off to the left. This thing is pretty nippy.

Now we're on this country road. It's fairly straight, so I keep my foot down.

Then we hear sirens.

I go a little bit faster. The trees and the hedges are flying past. It's like the middle of the countryside here, even though we are just a few miles outside Bexton. I slow down. There's a crossroads coming up and I don't want to miss it. Devil and me planned out this route some time last week. I know the turning is here somewhere. Near a tree…there it is. I try and turn in but I get the angle wrong and I'm nearly in the ditch. Now I have to back up. Devil looks interested now.

Ally Kennen, *Beserk* (2007)

**2 a)** What effect is created by the longer paragraphs (1 and 4)? Why has the writer included longer paragraphs here?
   **b)** What is the effect of the shorter paragraphs (2 and 3)? Why has the writer chosen to keep these as one or two sentences?
   **c)** Explain why you think it is effective to include variety in the length of paragraphs. Consider how this might work in viewpoint writing, as well as narrative.
**3** Look back at the plan you made for the writing task in Activity 1.
   Select one of your more detailed sections and write it, but make sure you split it into more than one paragraph. Aim for some variety in paragraph length.

Read this student's opening about a job experience that didn't go according to plan.

**What do you think of her use of connectives?**

In the Easter holidays my mum turned to me and said, 'Why don't you think about getting a weekend job?'. I was shocked. 'Well, you are fifteen now. It's time you did some work.' So, I started thinking. Maybe she was right. It would be quite cool to have a job and it would really help me to save up for the new phone I wanted. The idea of the hairdressers down the road sprang to mind! I'd seen an ad in their window last week so I called the owner and she said she'd give me a trial on Saturday. I was dead excited. I've always loved doing my friends' hair and maybe this could be an actual career for me. Anyway, Saturday came around quickly and soon I was stood outside Snippets trying to stay calm. The windows were all steamed up so I didn't see until I got inside how busy it was. In the shop, there were six mirrors around the room with a chair in front of each one. In each chair was a customer having their hair done. The noise of the hairdryers and the voices of all the people was horrendous! I suddenly felt very hot and bothered. The room was hot and smelly from all the products being sprayed around and the floor was covered with other people's hair. I was about to back out quietly, when there was a shout from the back of the room…

This student would be awarded a Grade 4 for the general standard of the writing. However, there are no paragraphs at all.

Decide where you would put the paragraphs, for maximum effect.

## 2 Making links within paragraphs

Writers also use connectives to link sentences and ideas **within** paragraphs. They can be used in a variety of different ways depending on the purpose and topic of a source.

## Practising for success

Read this text.

> He looked around the room that was to be his home for the next six months. In the corner was a rickety looking metal-framed bed. It was covered with a faded grey duvet cover; underneath this was a sheet that Jim supposed had once been white. To the left of the bed was a table and chair — both metal and both grey. There was a small pile of paper on the table and a single blue biro, which was the most colourful thing in the room. The floor underneath the table was scratched; Jim guessed this was from the chair legs being pushed over it as previous occupiers had sat and written — what? — at the desk. Jim sighed and looked up at the single bare light bulb hanging from the ceiling. The only other thing giving off any light was the tiny, barred window above the bed. Home sweet home, he thought sadly.

## ACTIVITY 1

**1** The writer has used lots of words and phrases here that tell us where things are in relation to one another. These help the reader to picture the place more clearly.

Write down the words/phrases that help to do this. For example:

*In the corner. It was covered …*

Look at this picture.

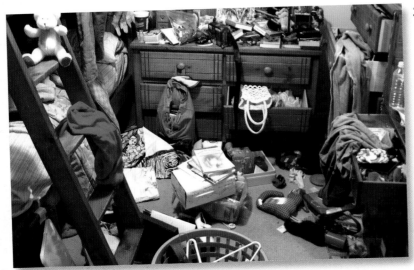

**2 a)** Make a list of all the things you can see in the room. Remember to add some description like in the passage on the previous page ('rickety looking metal-framed bed'). For example:

*wooden ladder, covered in bits and pieces, leading to top bunk*

**b)** Now, write a description, adding a range of connectives to link these items and show where they are in relation to one another. Use the connectives to take your reader on a virtual journey around the room.

**3** The connectives you have just been working with are all to do with 'place'.

**a)** How many connectives can you think of that are related to 'time'?

**b)** Use your list of time connectives to write an outline of a typical weekend for you.

- **On Saturday** I wake up late. **After** breakfast, I have a shower and **then** get dressed.

Time connectives

Read the following extract. It is taken from an article about the musician Calvin Harris.

A 'time' connective →

In June 2011, Harris released "Bounce" as the first single of his third studio album. It was followed by "Feel So Close" that became Harris' first solo entry on the Billboard Hot 100 in the U.S., peaking at number twelve. For the new album, Harris collaborated with the likes of Ellie Goulding, Ne-Yo, Rihanna, Kelis and Florence Welch. "Feel So Close" won Best Electronic Video at the 2012 MTV Video Music Awards where he was made the house DJ. Harris also won Video of the Year for his Rihanna-collaborative track "We Found Love" at the awards show. After months of promotional efforts, the album "18 Months" hit the stores October 26, 2012 via Columbia Records.

www.aceshowbiz.com

**4 a)** Find and list all the connectives that link ideas and information.
**b)** This extract tells about some of the successes that Calvin Harris has had. Think about something that you have done well. Write a paragraph about your achievement. Use a range of connectives to link and sequence your ideas.

**Boost your grade** ⬆

Read this extract from a student's Grade 5 response. She was writing about where she lives.

> By far, the most breathtaking thing about our town is the sea front. I love nothing more than finishing school and heading down to the beach with my friends – whatever the weather. Usually we just sit on the rocks and chat, but sometimes we'll take a ball for a kick around on the sand. On sunny days, we might even go for a paddle! Even in the winter, we bundle up and sit under the pier and watch the waves crashing violently into each other. It's always fun and refreshing – rain or shine.

1 How well organised is her writing?
2 Has she used connectives to link her ideas?
3 Do they work well?

Produce one paragraph of your own, about where you live, that matches this standard and has the same high quality features.

## Test yourself

You read an opinion letter in your local newspaper that says: 'School children today are getting more and more rude and disrespectful. Teenagers need to learn some manners!'

Write a letter back to the newspaper, giving your point of view in relation to this. Remember to:

- plan out your ideas carefully before you start writing
- use a range of connectives to link ideas between and within paragraphs.

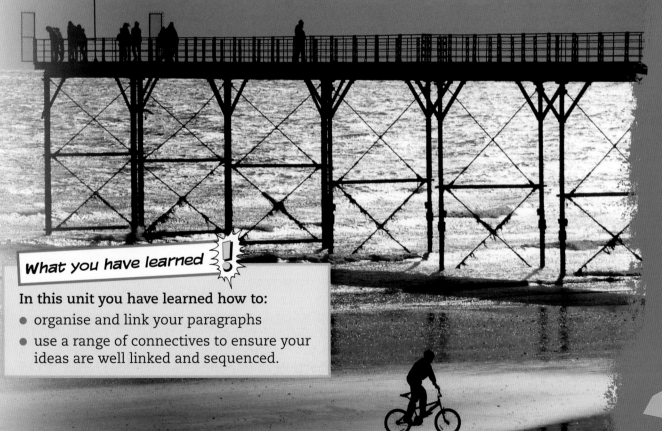

**What you have learned** !

**In this unit you have learned how to:**

- organise and link your paragraphs
- use a range of connectives to ensure your ideas are well linked and sequenced.

# Vocabulary and crafting

**In this unit you will focus on how to:**
⇨ vary your vocabulary effectively
⇨ use similes, metaphors and alliteration
⇨ use linguistic techniques to express a point of view.

**What this unit involves**

This unit focuses on one of your priorities when responding to writing tasks: you need to use a range of **vocabulary** and **linguistic devices**.

## 1 Using a range of vocabulary

Using a wide range of vocabulary will help to make your writing more descriptive, detailed and engaging – and improve your marks.

## Practising for success

Read this extract from the horror novel *Bec* by Darren Shan.

> A boy's screams pierce the silence of the night and the village explodes into life. Warriors are already racing towards him by the time I whirl from my watching point near the gate. Torches are flung into the darkness.
>
> Darren Shan, *Bec* (2013)

### ACTIVITY 1

**1** Find and write down the verbs that the writer has used.

Discussion point

**2** Working with a friend, decide why each verb works well. Look at what **noun** each **verb** relates to and think about the effect that is created.

For example:

> The verb 'pierced' is used to describe the boy's scream. This makes it seem like the scream was really loud and sudden — it is sharp and shocking.

Examiner comment

People often think of adjectives being the 'describing words' but verbs can be just as descriptive. Verbs too can create action and emotion.

**3** Read the extract again. Notice that – besides common words (like 'the', 'and') – the writer has not repeated any vocabulary. He finds an alternative each time:

...*the silence of the* night – ...*flung into the* darkness

Now read this student response. It would be awarded a Grade 3 but uses simple vocabulary and there is not a wide range.

> A *big, scary house* stood *over the children. The* big*, black door* looked *like a* scary *open mouth.* Big *windows* stood *on either side of the black door and* looked *out at them like a pair of* scary *eyes.*

**4 a)** Rewrite this passage to improve the grade. Change some of the highlighted words to add a greater range of vocabulary.
   **b)** Edit your writing further to add some additional words to increase the description and effect.

   A *huge ghastly house towered* **intimidatingly** *over the* **lost children**.

**5** Now, rewrite each of these sentences. Identify the verb or verbs in each one and change them to create a greater impact or effect.

   *The cat jumped onto the high garden wall.*

   *He sat down at his desk and wrote the essay.*

   *Huge branches hung down from the old gnarled tree.*

   *Flocks of seagulls cried out impatiently for their dinner.*

   *The fire alarm bell rang; the teacher jumped to her feet.*

This extract is from a novel by Stephen King, who writes horror stories. Here, he describes an old house.

Its steep roof overhung the front porch like a beetling brow. The boards of the porch were splintery and warped. Shutters which might once have been green leaned **askew** beside the glassless windows; ancient curtains still hung in some of these, dangling like strips of dead skin.

{ askew means twisted, lopsided }

Stephen King, *The Dark Tower: The Waste Lands* (1992)

**6** What is the mood in this extract? Which words help to set the mood? Copy and complete this table.

| WORDS | EFFECT ON MOOD |
|---|---|
| splintery and warped | suggest age, decay and unpleasantness |
| | |
| | |

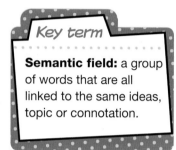

**Key term**

**Semantic field:** a group of words that are all linked to the same ideas, topic or connotation.

Many of the words suggest decay and great age. When a number of words are placed together like this, it is called a **semantic field**.

When you are writing to describe, a semantic field can prove powerful.

**7** Imagine you have to describe a primary school playground.

Select words you might use in your response, under the following headings:
- Fun/games
- Lack of space

Boost your grade

Write a paragraph using some of those words, to create the atmosphere of a busy playground. Try not to repeat any words. You might choose to focus on one semantic field from the list above or combine the two.

## 2 Linguistic devices

Writers often use similes, metaphors and alliteration.

## Practising for success

Read this poem by Alfred Lord Tennyson. It is describing an eagle:

He clasps the **crag** with crooked hands;
Close to the sun in lonely lands
Ring'd with the **azure** world, he stands.

The wrinkled sea beneath him crawls;
He watches from his mountain walls,
And like a thunderbolt he falls.

Alfred, Lord Tennyson, *The Eagle* (1851)

**crag** is a steep cliff
**azure** is blue

## ACTIVITY 1

**1** Find and write down an example of:

**a) alliteration**
**b) simile**
**c) metaphor**.

**2** For each linguistic device you have found, explain why you think this use of language is effective here. How does it help to describe?

*The metaphor 'wrinkled sea' is effective because it helps me to picture the sea from above. I can imagine that there are lots of waves and that it is quite choppy. It is like wrinkles on someone's forehead.*

**3** Write your own description of an eagle, using your own simile, metaphor and alliteration. You can produce a poem or a paragraph of writing.

Of course, linguistic devices are used in most forms of writing – including the responses you will have to produce in the exam.

Look closely at this image.

**4** Think of some descriptive phrases you could use to write about this tiger. Write down at least one example of:

- alliteration
- simile
- metaphor.

Remembering to vary your vocabulary throughout, now craft your descriptive phrases further into a complete paragraph of writing. For example:

*He is like a golden hunting machine, with murderous eyes and slow, slick movements...*

> **Key terms**
>
> **Alliteration:** when the same letter or sound occurs at the start of words that are next to or close to each other.
>
> **Simile:** a phrase that compares one thing to another using the words 'as' or 'like'.
>
> **Metaphor:** when you use a metaphor you are also comparing. However, you do not use 'like' or 'as'. It is something that is not literally true.

Read the opening to this student's short story about a journey into the mountains.

**1** What do you think about her choice of vocabulary?
**2** Can you find examples of any linguistic devices?

> Over in the distance, the majestic mountains stood proudly in the autumn sunlight. It was a beautiful day for a hike and there was not a single cloud in the brilliant blue sky. In fact, even though it was September, the golden sun was shining brightly and warming the heads and shoulders of the group of friends.
>
> 'Let's go!' cried Jess excitedly. She ran ahead of the group with her arms out to the side like a bird's wings. She could feel the cool breeze on her face and it made her smile.

This student would receive marks from the Grade 5 band because:

- the chosen words are effective and successful in describing and setting the scene
- the vocabulary is varied
- there is successful use of a range of linguistic devices.

**3** Think of two people you have met at a party or football match. They must be very different. Write two detailed paragraphs, describing them.
In both descriptions, make sure you use:
- varied vocabulary – remember the power of semantic fields
- similes, metaphor and alliteration.

## 3 Crafting your writing to express a viewpoint

When you are writing to express a viewpoint, you can use the same techniques. There are also additional ones that are often used to make the writing more effective.

## Practising for success

Read this extract in which the writer is giving his viewpoint on a place he has visited: Blackpool. He selects his details carefully to create an overall effect.

Bryson uses a metaphor to create exaggeration

> It was the illuminations that had brought me there. I had been hearing and reading about them for so long that I was genuinely keen to see them. So, after securing a room in a modest guesthouse on a back street, I hastened to the front in a sense of some expectation. Well, all I can say is that Blackpool's illuminations are nothing if not splendid, and they are not splendid. There is, of course, always a danger of disappointment when you finally encounter something you have wanted to see for a long time, but in terms of letdown it would be hard to exceed Blackpool's light show. I thought there would be lasers sweeping the sky, strobe lights tattooing the clouds and other gasp-making dazzlements. Instead →

> there was just a rumbling procession of old trams decorated as rocket ships or Christmas crackers, and several miles of **paltry** decorations on lampposts. I suppose if you had never seen electricity in action, it would be pretty breathtaking, but I'm not even sure of that. It all just seemed tacky and inadequate on a rather grand scale, like Blackpool itself.
>
> Bill Bryson, *Notes From a Small Island* (1995)

Using second person pronouns to address the reader directly is an effective technique for viewpoint writing

{ **paltry** is miserable or pathetic }

Bryson's choice of words help to convey his viewpoint: 'hastened' and 'expectation' suggest he is **excited**; 'tacky' and 'inadequate' help to describe his disappointment.

## ACTIVITY 1

1 What does the writer think about Blackpool?

2 Find and write down some **emotive words** that suggest his feelings.

The writer uses exaggeration to emphasise his viewpoint.

An example of this is:

'...*in terms of letdown it would be hard to exceed Blackpool's light show.*'

3 Find another example of exaggeration and explain how it adds to the writer's viewpoint.

The writer has also used **sarcasm**.

*Blackpool's illuminations are nothing if not splendid, and they are not splendid.*

4 Find another example of sarcasm in the source.

The carefully selected detail, the emotive words, the exaggeration and the sarcasm all help to promote the writer's viewpoint.

5 Think about a place you have visited that has not lived up to your expectations.

Give your opinion of it, using the techniques you have just been examining.

**125**

This is from an advertising leaflet for Sefton Skate Park:

> Feeling bored these school holidays? Looking to meet some new friends? Want to take up an awesome new sport? Head down to Sefton Skate Park this Saturday for some serious fun. With five different ramps, amazing grinding rails and a powerful floodlight, this really is the place to be — day or night!

**6** Notice the different types of sentences the writer has used to express their viewpoint about the skate park. Find and record an example of each one:

**a)** rhetorical question

**b)** exclamation

**c)** sentence with a list of three, to make it seem there is much on offer.

What effect does each one have here?

Examiner comment

Just as emotive language, similes, metaphors and alliteration might well be appropriate devices to use in a response in which you give your views; so exaggeration, sarcasm, rhetorical questions, lists of three and exclamations might well be appropriate in descriptive or narrative responses.

**7** Write the opening of a leaflet to attract visitors to the place you live. Obviously express positive views. Use a range of linguistic techniques. Underline and label each one as you go, and try to use a different one each time.

Read this extract from a student's letter. It is expressing his viewpoint about the internet.

**1** What do you notice about the vocabulary and linguistic devices he has chosen to use?

Rhetorical question ⟋                                    Casual expression ⟍

> Why do so many adults criticise the internet? It's great. It gives us information, entertainment and even books to read. Just because we spend hours on the internet doesn't mean we are stupid. We are talking to our friends. It's stretching our minds all the time. Everyone should love it, not knock it.

Simple sentence, but with list of three

More simple sentences                    Simple comparison

This student is working at a Grade 3 level. Notice how simple everything seems.

**2** Produce a much better justification of the internet, using the techniques you have been practising.

## Test yourself

Write the opening to a short story that takes place in this setting.

Remember to include a range of vocabulary and linguistic devices, to enrich your ideas.

In this unit you have learned how to:

● use a range of words and linguistic devices to describe, narrate or express a viewpoint.

# Using effective punctuation

## What this unit involves

This unit will guide you through how to use a range of punctuation accurately and for effect. You will receive marks for punctuation in your Section B answers, as well as for spelling and punctuation.

**In this unit you will:**

⇨ learn how to use a range of accurate punctuation in your writing

⇨ experiment with using punctuation to create effects.

## Precise skills focus

⇨ using full stops, capital letters, exclamation marks and question marks to punctuate sentences

⇨ using commas to separate parts of sentences

⇨ using apostrophes

⇨ using speech marks and other punctuation for direct speech

⇨ using brackets, dashes, colons and semi-colons for impact and effect.

## 1 Using punctuation accurately

Being able to punctuate sentences must be a priority: otherwise, your work is hard to understand.

## Practising for success

### Commas

Read this passage. This extract is set in a different sort of world.

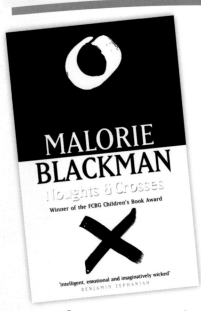

> I moved the cursor over to SHUT DOWN and clicked, yawning as I waited for my PC to switch off. It seemed to be taking forever tonight. At last, there was a clunk and the screen went black. I pressed the button to switch off my monitor and switched off the loudspeakers. Now for a quick drink and then bed. First day of school tomorrow. I groaned at the thought. School! I'd see all my friends again and we'd have the usual conversations, about the places we'd visited, the films we'd seen, the parties we'd posed at — and before long it would be like we'd never been away from school at all. The same old faces, the same old teachers, the same old, same old! But that wasn't strictly true, was it? At least tomorrow would be a bit different from the start of every other new term. Four **noughts**, including Callum, were starting at my school. Maybe he'd even be in my class.
>
> Malorie Blackman, *Noughts and Crosses* (2001)

{ **noughts** are what the author uses to call white children }

## ACTIVITY 1

Full stops are used to end a sentence, and the next sentence then begins with a capital letter.

1 Can you think of other uses for a capital letter? What examples can you find in this extract?

What other punctuation marks could mark the end of a sentence? What examples can you find in this extract?

2 Read the first sentence carefully and this time notice the <u>comma</u>.

This is a sophisticated use of a comma. It separates two verbs that are right next to each other. Read the sentence aloud; you will notice that you need to take a pause here, so the sentence makes sense. The comma signals this.

Commas are also used to add information to a main **clause**. The part that is added is called a **subordinate clause**. These are in blue below.

For example:

*Because I had toothache, I screamed all night.*

*My mother woke up, which meant I was in trouble.*

*My dad, who doesn't like to be disturbed, threw his empty beer can at me.*

Commas are also used to separate the parts in a list – though the final parts are joined with 'and'.

For example:

*I had an angry dad, a panicking mother and a screaming baby sister in my room.*

*I ended up going to the dentist's, having a filling, being late for school and spending all day with a headache.*

3 a) Identify where commas have been used in the passage from *Noughts and Crosses*. Can you explain how they have been used?
   b) Write two sentences using commas to separate the parts of a list.

Commas also separate details of 'how', 'where' or 'when' from the main clause and follow a connective. For example:

*Quickly, I grabbed my bag.*

*In the distance, I could see the bus.*

*In a matter of moments, it would arrive – or so I thought.*

*However, all was not as it seemed.*

**Examiner comment**

Exclamation marks are used to express strong feelings. However, for this to have the most impact they must be used sparingly. As a general rule, only use exclamation marks once or twice in each written response – and **never** double them up!

**Key terms**

**Clause:** a main clause makes sense on its own.

**Subordinate clause:** a subordinate clause will not make sense on its own.

**c)** Write four sentences, to show you understand these four uses. (Try to make them into a little story.)

**4** Write a paragraph about your first day back at school after a holiday, using commas in at least three different ways.

## Apostrophes

ACTIVITY 2

**1** Find and write down three words from the first day at school extract that use an apostrophe. Can you see why an apostrophe was needed in each of these words?

One use of an apostrophe is used to show **omission**.

**2** Rewrite the following sentences by contracting the words in bold and adding an apostrophe for omission where it is needed.

For example:

*I **cannot** stand that film!* – *I **can't** stand that film!*

- *I **have** always said that you are a great dancer.*
- *It **has** been raining non-stop since Tuesday and I do not like it!*
- *You **will** never guess where we are going on the History trip this year.*

**3** Find other words in the sentences above that could be contracted with an apostrophe for omission.

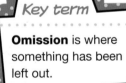

**Key term**

**Omission** is where something has been left out.

> **Examiner comment**
>
> **Your** and **you're** are common errors in exam answers. If you are unsure about which one to use, think: would the sentence still make sense if I changed it to 'you are'? If the answer is yes, you need 'you're' with the apostrophe. The same thing goes for its/it's – if you could say 'it is' instead, you need an apostrophe.

Apostrophes can also be used for **possession**, to show that something belongs to somebody.

Mistakes are often made with apostrophes around the letter **s**.

If the person or thing that owns something is singular, add an apostrophe and an **s**, (you can do this even if that word ends in **s**).

For example: *No matter how hard he tried, he couldn't beat James's top score.*

If the person or thing that owns something is a plural that does not end in **s**, add an apostrophe and an **s**.

For example: *There were children's toys strewn all over the playground.*

If the person or thing that owns something is plural ending in **s**, add an apostrophe after the **s**.

For example: *A sale for ladies' shoes was being held on the ground floor.*

**4** Add an apostrophe to the right word in these sentences:

- In the morning, that **cats bowl** is always empty!
- Suddenly, the **bosss shadow** fell over him.
- My parents stories about me as a baby are so annoying!
- In the Olympics, I thought the mens swimming was exciting to watch.
- In the darkness, the buses lights are like beacons.

**5** Write the opening to a story about a trip you have been on recently, taking care to punctuate your sentences accurately. Think carefully about where:

- capital letters are needed
- apostrophes are needed
- full stops are needed
- a question mark is needed
- commas are needed
- an exclamation mark could be used.

## 3 Using punctuation for direct speech

Direct speech is a great device to use if you are writing a narrative in Paper 1. Dialogue can help to create characters and it can speed up the plot. You might also use direct speech or quotations in in a description or your viewpoint writing for Paper 2.

## Practising for success

Read this passage and notice the rules for punctuating speech.

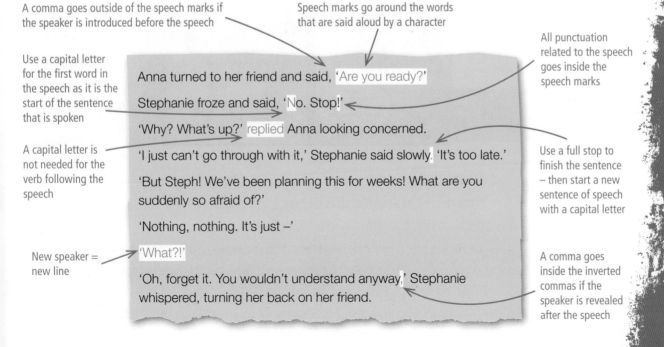

A comma goes outside of the speech marks if the speaker is introduced before the speech

Speech marks go around the words that are said aloud by a character

All punctuation related to the speech goes inside the speech marks

Use a capital letter for the first word in the speech as it is the start of the sentence that is spoken

A capital letter is not needed for the verb following the speech

New speaker = new line

Use a full stop to finish the sentence – then start a new sentence of speech with a capital letter

A comma goes inside the inverted commas if the speaker is revealed after the speech

Anna turned to her friend and said, 'Are you ready?'

Stephanie froze and said, 'No. Stop!'

'Why? What's up?' replied Anna looking concerned.

'I just can't go through with it,' Stephanie said slowly. 'It's too late.'

'But Steph! We've been planning this for weeks! What are you suddenly so afraid of?'

'Nothing, nothing. It's just –'

'What?!'

'Oh, forget it. You wouldn't understand anyway,' Stephanie whispered, turning her back on her friend.

## ACTIVITY 1

**1** Write a short conversation linked to the piece of writing you did in the last activity about a trip you have been on. Be sure to use accurate speech punctuation.

Look at this short extract from a graphic novel.

The extract is from a Sherlock Holmes story:

- Eliza has been taken in and needs to be looked after
- The Irregulars are street children used by Sherlock as secret agents
- Wiggins is their leader
- the children thought they were going to have to leave.

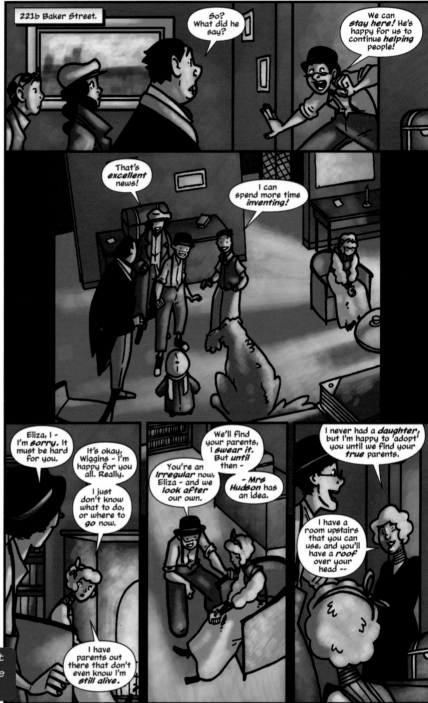

*Sherlock Holmes The Baker Street Irregulars: The adventure of the missing detective (2011)*

**2** Write the story of what is happening, including some direct speech. You might start like this Grade 5 student:

The group of friends stood around, nervously. The red walls of the room seemed to be closing in on them as they waited for the news. Claire paced around clicking her fingers.

'So, what did he say?' asked John, as Joe burst in.

'We can stay here!' shouted Joe. 'He's happy for us to continue helping people!'

**Boost your grade** ⬆

This student has continued the dialogue. Notice how she has used direct speech:

Speech marks are used around the words that are spoken

Exclamation marks are used sparingly to show character emotions

Capital letters are used for new sentences and names

> 'Oh Mrs Hudson that would be fantastic! Thank you,' Cried Eliza.
>
> 'Now, that's all settled then.' Said Joe.
>
> 'Great! Eliza can get comfortable at Mrs Hudson's too then. Where shall we go to celebrate,' smiled John.

Rewrite this section of speech, making sure it is all accurate and raising it to Grade 5. Change it so that the speakers are put in different positions within the sentence (e.g. in the middle of what is said, or at the beginning, or before the words spoken).

**Assessment comment**

This student would be awarded a Grade 4 for punctuation. Although speech marks have been used, some of the other elements of punctuation let the response down.

## 4 Using a range of punctuation for control and effect

If you can use a range of punctuation with confidence, you will add interesting effects and you will show that you can control your writing.

### Dashes, brackets and ellipses

Read this extract from a movie review:

> Let's take a look now at the must-see animation of the year: Big Hero 6.
>
> **Big Hero 6** is an action-packed comedy-adventure about robotics prodigy Hiro Hamada. Hiro learns to harness his genius thanks to his brilliant brother Tadashi and their like-minded friends: adrenaline junkie Go Go Tamago, neatnik Wasabi, chemistry whiz Honey Lemon and fanboy Fred. When a devastating turn of events catapults them into the midst of a dangerous plot unfolding in the streets of San Fransokyo, Hiro turns to his closest companion – a robot named Baymax – and transforms the group into a band of high-tech heroes determined to solve the mystery.
>
> Nobody who has seen **The Incredibles** (Pixar) or **Bolt** (Disney) should be in any doubt that animated superheroes can work superbly on the big screen. So it should come as no surprise that the **Mouse House's** first venture proper into comic-book territory, **Big Hero 6**, is picking up plenty of buzz ahead of its UK release in January (November for North America). US bloggers – who saw 25 minutes of footage earlier this week – reckon it could be a frontrunner for next year's best animated film Oscar…

## ACTIVITY 1

**1 a)** Find an example of a **dash** in the movie review. Why has the writer chosen to include a dash here?

  **b)** Find an example of brackets in the review. Why has the writer chosen to include brackets here?

  **c)** Why is there an **ellipsis** at the end?

### Key terms

**Dash:** used to show an interruption from the main sentence, so that the writer can include additional information. If the interruption comes at the end of a sentence a single dash is used.

*There's too much reality TV these days – I'm sick of seeing people baking, cooking and building houses!*

If the interruption comes in the middle of a sentence, a pair of dashes is used.

*Last night – at about eight o'clock – I sat down to watch the TV.*

Here, the dashes replace commas

**Ellipsis:** three dots (…) which suggest there is more to come, leaving the reader to imagine what comes next.

Brackets always appear in pairs. Use them to interrupt the main sentence so that you can add some additional information or chat to the reader through an aside. For example:

*Stormbreaker (a best seller) was published in 2005.*

*Season seven (can you believe it?) of Game of Thrones is in the making.*

**2** Write a paragraph, giving your views on your favourite band or TV show. Use dashes, brackets and an ellipsis.

## Colons and semi-colons

If you use colons and semi-colons correctly, you will really impress the examiner.

**Colons** follow a general statement and introduce a list that adds extra detail:

*She is beautiful: dark flowing hair, green eyes and a button nose.*

*There was nothing more to say: the boat had sunk, the men had died and all was lost.*

**Semi-colons** have two uses:

1 To separate the parts of a complicated list:

*For breakfast, I eat cereal, toast and eggs (simple list, using a comma).*

*For breakfast, I eat any cereal we have in the cupboard; lightly buttered toast with jam; and eggs that have been boiled for exactly four minutes. (complicated list, using semi-colons)*

*I love Shabnum, because of her wit and good humour; Tejinder, because of her knowledge and intellect; and Eloise, because of her beauty. (complicated list, using semi-colons)*

2 To join two separate sentences into one, if the ideas in each are closely related.

*I hate Tuesdays; we have double maths in the afternoon.*

*The end of the match must come soon; I can't take any more.*

## ACTIVITY 2

**1** Write a description of what you like to do on a typical weekend. Include at least one colon and a semi-colon.

Read this student's description of her weekend:

> *Last week I took my little sister along to the cinema to watch the latest Disney release Frozen. I have to say that I was not disappointed and neither was she. The special effects were amazing and the animation was great and the soundtrack was good and very catchy! I would sum this movie up in one word breath-taking.*

This comes from a Grade 3 candidate. There is some variety of punctuation, but not much. Generally, this just relies on full-stops to help the reader.

Rewrite the response, improving the punctuation. If you can, add:

- a comma
- a pair of brackets
- a dash
- a colon and semi-colon
- an ellipsis.

You might wish to change some of the writing slightly – for example, by removing some of the 'and's.

**Examiner comment**

It's a good idea to include mention of colons, semi-colons and other punctuation marks in your essay plan – that way, you remember to include them.

## Test yourself

You see this advertisement on the school website:

Enter our creative writing competition for the chance to win a family weekend away.

Write a description of a holiday or trip you have been on.

Or

Write the opening to a short story about a special celebration.

Remember to use a range of punctuation, including speech marks, accurately in words and sentences. Experiment with using punctuation like dashes, brackets, colons and semi-colons to add more control and effect.

**What you have learned**

In this unit, you have learned:
- how to punctuate sentences accurately
- how to use the apostrophe of omission and possession
- how to punctuate direct speech
- how to make your writing more effective and precise by using a range of punctuation.

# Improving sentences and grammar

**In this unit you will:**

⇨ learn about the range of sentences you can use in your writing
⇨ experiment with varying sentences for impact and effect.

This unit will guide you through how to use a range of sentence types and structures accurately and for effect. You will be marked on this in your Section B answers, so sentences are important.

## Precise skills focus

⇨ long and short sentences
⇨ simple, compound and complex sentences
⇨ rhetorical question and exclamations
⇨ lists, contrasts and repetitive structures for effect.

## 1 Using a range of sentence lengths, structures and types

Using a range of sentences will help you make your writing more interesting. You should aim to include a range of sentence lengths, structures and types in every piece of Section B writing.

## Practising for success

### Sentence length

You will need to vary your sentence lengths appropriately for what you are writing. You might need long sentences for detailed description; or to clarify a viewpoint.

A short sentence can surprise the reader or give a sudden emphasis.

This was written by a Grade 5 student:

> The worst thing was when I was told that my opinion was irrelevant because I am still at school and that, anyway, I should simply do as I'm told because I am only a girl. I was appalled.

### ACTIVITY 1

**1** Think of a time when you were surprised or delighted. Write a long sentence describing the event, followed by a short one that indicates your surprise or delight.

The same girl wrote this:

> It was lovely to be outside again, as the hall had become hotter and hotter as the exam went on and, in fact, quite a few students had to be taken out for fresh air and to get a glass of water. It was wonderful outside. I could breathe again.

**2** In three sentences, write a description of a time when you were ill. Make one or two of the sentences short, to create an effect (upset, relief, horror …).

## Simple, complex and compound sentences

Examiners check that you are using a mixture of simple, complex and compound sentences.

**Simple sentence:** made up of just one main clause.

> *I love swimming.*

**Compound sentence:** made up of two or more main clauses, usually joined by **and**, **but**, **or**.

> *We went to the beach last weekend and we had an ice cream.*

**Complex sentence:** made up of one main clause plus one or more subordinate clauses.

> *When I read a book, I always lose track of the time because I get so engrossed.*

---

### Key terms

**Main clause:** can stand alone as a complete sentence; it makes sense on its own.

> *I bought a new pair of jeans.*

**Subordinate clause:** will not make sense on its own; it needs a main clause in a sentence for it to make sense.

> *Because I ripped a hole in my old ones*

> *I bought a new pair of jeans because I ripped hole in my old ones.*

---

Here, the Grade 5 student mixes her different sentence types well:

Compound sentence

> I was a bundle of nerves but then the exam results were excellent.
> As my dad said, I needn't have worried. Hard work always pays off.

Complex sentence          Simple sentence

**139**

## ACTIVITY 2

**1** Write a simple sentence about your favourite hobby or interest.

**2** Add another main clause to make this simple sentence into a compound sentence. For example:

*I enjoy playing on my Xbox but I don't like playing platform games.*

**3** Add a subordinate clause to your original simple sentence to create a complex sentence.

For example:

*I enjoy playing on my Xbox, to relax and prepare for more work.*

Experiment with writing a subordinate clause at different points in the sentence. Would it work better at the beginning, or the end? Could it go in the middle, so you **embed** it?

*I enjoy playing Halo, which is a sci-fi shooting game, on my Xbox.*

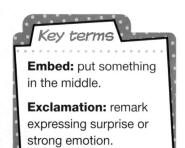

**Key terms**

**Embed:** put something in the middle.

**Exclamation:** remark expressing surprise or strong emotion.

### Questions and exclamations

Used sparingly, rhetorical questions and **exclamations** can enliven your writing.

This is taken from a letter to a national newspaper:

People talk about the fact that Scotland should be independent. Sometimes they say the same about Wales. However, why do they overlook the fact that there are more people in Yorkshire than in Wales and New Zealand put together? Why does no one point out that there are more acres in Yorkshire than words in the Bible? Why don't people remember that in the 2012 Olympics, Yorkshire did better than Jamaica, Spain, South Africa and Brazil? Surely, Yorkshire deserves to be a country in its own right!

## ACTIVITY 3

**1** Write a short paragraph giving your view(s) on England. Include at least one rhetorical question and an exclamation.

**Key term**

**Standard English** avoids slang and uses proper sentences – each one should have a verb (a doing word), e.g. She**'s been** famous for ages. However, I still **love** Taylor Swift.

The only time you might not fulfil this rule is if you are using a short sentence for effect, e.g. 'Appalling!'; 'Totally hopeless.'

**2** Notice the use of accent and dialect in this student's response.
Rewrite it in Standard English.

> Yo! Listen up. I ain't gonna stand here and be, like, I really wanna do
> this exam, right? But, like, we just gotta get on with it right? So, I
> reckon if we all just get our heads down we'll get it done and it'll be cool
> right? There ain't no-one that can do it but you, so just get on with it!

**Examiner comment**

Throughout, remember to always write in **Standard English**.

**Boost your grade** ↗

With a partner, read through this extract from a student's short story.

**1** What do you notice about her sentences?
**2** Do you think there is a good range?
**3** How do you think she could improve her sentence variety and control?

> I wanted to walk across the rope so I scrumped up the ladder. I looked down and it was fair high
> so I thought that I can't do it, but then I thought that I can do it so I took a deep breath. Quite scared,
> like. I put my foot on the rope and I looked straight forward. It was hard to keep my balance so I had to
> work hard.

**Assessment comment**

This student would receive marks from the Grade 2 band because:

- there is not a good range of sentences – notice how almost all begin with 'I' and they are all compound sentences with 'so' used repeatedly
- it is mainly in the past tense ('wanted') but sometimes slips into the present tense ('can') so the writing is not always controlled
- it's not all in Standard English – 'quite scared, like' – and poor vocabulary: 'scrumped up', 'fair high'.

Read through the opening to this student's short story:

> It was a grey day, where the sun was really trying to push through the cloud but couldn't make it.
> I was hanging around after school – with Robbo, and Clarky. As usual, we had nothing to do. Nothing.
>    Suddenly Robbo looked up and shouted, 'Oh yes!'
>    'What is it?' I asked, waking up from my boredom. Looking up, all I could see was a bit of scaffolding
> left over from some building work they'd been doing on the old block of flats. 'What?' I demanded again.
>    Robbo grinned, 'Come on boys. I've got an idea.' When Robbo gets that look in his eyes,
> it's best to turn around and walk away. However, I was curious and bored.
>    I looked at Clarky who also looked a bit worried. 'It's ok, let's just see what he has to say.'

**4** This is clearly better. Make a list of all the things that are good about the sentences.

## 2 Varying sentences for effect

As well as using a range of sentences to add interest, you can also use specific techniques to create impact and effect.

### Practising for success

Read this extract from a speech by rugby coach Jim Telfer to his team before a big match.

> They don't respect you. They don't rate you. The only way to be rated is to stick one on them, to get right up in their faces and turn them back, knock them back. Outdo what they do. Outjump them, **outscrum** them, **outruck** them, **outdrive** them, **outtackle** them, until they're sick of you.
>
> Remember the pledges you made. Remember how you depend on each other at every phase, teams within teams, scrums, lineouts, ruck ball, tackles.
>
> They are better than you've played against so far. They are better individually or they wouldn't be there. So it's an awesome task you have and it will only be done if everybody commits themself now.

**outscrum, outruck, outdrive, outtackle** are all rugby terms about driving the team on and forcing opponents back

Jim Telfer (2009)

### ACTIVITY 1

**1** Find at least one example of each of the effective sentence techniques listed in the table on page 143.

For each technique and example, explain the effect that is created. Copy and complete the table with your ideas.

| EFFECTIVE SENTENCE TECHNIQUE | EXAMPLE(S) | EFFECT THAT IS CREATED |
|---|---|---|
| Repetitive structures | They don't respect you. They don't rate you | |
| Lists | | Provides different examples – it makes the audience think about how hard they have to work. |
| Commands | | |

Re-read the Jim Telfer speech. Notice how, even though he is talking to his players directly, he still speaks in Standard English.

2 Write the opening to a speech you might give to a group of friends before a big event – for example: a sports match, a school play, an exam.

Use repetition, a list and a command.

Now, read this extract from a famous speech by Nelson Mandela who was a black politician in South Africa. He worked to remove the barriers that existed between black and white people in his country and create a better life for African people.

Africans want to perform work which they are capable of doing, and not work which the government declares them to be capable of. Africans want to be allowed to live where they obtain work, and not be **endorsed** out of an area because they were not born there. Africans want to be allowed to own land in places where they work, and not to be **obliged** to live in rented houses which they can never call their own. Africans want to be part of the general population, and not confined to living in their own **ghettoes.**

Nelson Mandela (1964)

**endorsed** means something is imposed by law

**obliged** means forced

**ghettoes** are a slum area of a city where minority groups live

Mandela's speech also uses repetitive structures.

3 Write down the words that are repeated. Why do you think the writer has chosen to use repetition here?

The first half of the sentence tells us what Africans want in contrast to what they are currently getting, in the second half of the sentence

The writer also uses the sentence technique of contrasts:

*Africans want to perform work which they are capable of doing, and not work which the government declares them to be capable of.*

4 Write down another example of a **contrast** in the extract. Why do you think the writer has chosen to use contrasts? Think about the effect it might have on the reader.

5 Write a short paragraph about something that you feel needs changing in your school or community. Include contrasts in some of your sentences.

For example:

*The state of school dinners in this school is terrible! Young people want food that actually tastes good, not slop that doesn't look or taste like anything. We want choice, we don't want to be told what we have to eat every day.*

Let's now look at what you remember about sentences and making writing more effective.

Read this extract from the travel book *Himalaya* by Michael Palin.

foetal ball is the position a baby lies in inside the mother's womb.

augmented means made greater.

**Day Fifty Nine: Xangmu to Tingri**

Xangmu high street, quiet as the grave when we arrived, erupts into life at night. Sounds of shouting, drilling, thumping and banging drift, unhampered, through tightly closed windows and into my head. I pull all the blankets off the unoccupied bed next to me, curl up in a **foetal ball** and hope it will all just go away. It doesn't. It gets worse. The hissing, clunking, industrial sounds seem to be **augmented** by flashes and crackles. Can someone really be spot-welding out there at 12.15? The prospect of how exhausted I'll feel in the morning keeps me awake for at least another hour.

Wake at eight, but it's still pitch dark. In fact, it doesn't begin to get light for another half-hour. The government of China, in their wisdom, **decreed** that the whole country, wider than the United States, should only have one time zone. The further west you are the later daybreak comes.

{ **decreed** means ordered. }

Michael Palin, *Himalaya* (2004)

1  a) Find and write down an example of a short, snappy sentence. Why do you think the writer has chosen to use a short sentence at this point?

   b) Find and write down the most effective complex sentence. What effect does it have?

   c) There is more than one list here. How is each one used?

   d) How are we supposed to respond to the rhetorical question?

A Grade 5 student gave her opinion on a place she had visited. This is the opening:

> Darwen! What a terrible place to live. I admit that I haven't been there for some years, but you wouldn't want to go back again. The people are nice, but the streets are grim, grey and wet. You want to enjoy your time in a town, not be depressed all the time. It makes you miserable, it makes you long for somewhere better and it makes you appreciate all the other places you've visited. Don't you feel sorry for the people who live there? Stay away! That's my advice.

2  Identify all the different ways sentences are used here.

3  Write a paragraph of your own about a place you have visited, varying the sentences for effect.

## Test yourself

Remembering to be especially careful to vary your sentences, respond to this task:

**Describe the town or city in which you live.**

### What you have learned

In this unit you have learned how to:
- add variety to your writing through using different lengths, structures and types of sentences
- use a variety of sentence techniques for effect.

# Writing to describe

In this unit you will:
⇒ structure a description of a place, person and occasion
⇒ add detail and effective description to your writing
⇒ use speech to develop your descriptions.

**What this unit involves**

In Section B of Paper 1 you are likely to have the opportunity to write to describe. There are 40 marks available and you will have to complete the writing in 45 minutes.

## 1 How to start: structuring and adding impressive features

When you are writing to describe, it is important to structure your writing carefully. This lesson teaches you how to organise your ideas. You can then experiment with adding details, strong vocabulary and effective sentence structures to enhance your description.

### Practising for success

Read this extract. It is taken from a novel set in the future. In it, the main character is taken to her new home, the 'Pit', which is described in this extract. She is joining a new group called the Dauntless.

The first sentence in each paragraph tells us the topic or focus of that paragraph

Specific details are then given about this topic

'Pit' is the best word for it. It is an underground cavern so huge I can't see the other end of it from where I stand, at the bottom. Uneven rock walls rise several stories above my head. Built into the stone walls are places for food, clothing, supplies, leisure activities. Narrow paths and steps carved from rock connect them. There are no barriers to keep people from falling over the side.

A slant of orange light stretches across one of the rock walls. Forming the roof of the Pit are panes of glass and, above them, a building that lets in sunlight. It must have looked just like another city building when we passed it on the train.

Blue lanterns dangle at random intervals above the stone paths, similar to the ones that lit the Choosing ceremony room. They grow brighter as the sunlight dies.

Adjectives are used to add detail and description

Dauntless is the name given to a group of people in the novel who do brave and fearless things – like jump off moving trains!

People are everywhere, all dressed in black, all shouting and talking, expressive, gesturing. I don't see any elderly people in the crowd. Are there any old **Dauntless**? Do they not last that long, or are they just sent away when they can't jump off moving trains anymore?

A group of children run down a narrow path with no railing, so fast my heart pounds, and I want to scream at them to slow down before they get hurt.

Veronica Roth, *Divergent* (2013)

## Organisation

### ACTIVITY 1

**1 a)** Notice how each paragraph has a different topic or *thing* that is being described. Copy and complete a table like the one below to record the *thing* that is being described in each paragraph.

**b)** Now, look at the specific details that are given about that thing. Add your observations to the table.

| PARAGRAPH | TOPIC OR *THING* BEING DESCRIBED | DETAILS THAT ARE GIVEN ABOUT THIS THING |
|---|---|---|
| 1 | The pit | Underground cavern |
| | | Huge |
| | | Uneven rock walls |
| | | … |
| | | … |
| 2 | Light | Slanting |
| | | Orange |
| | | … |
| 3 | | |

**2** Create a five-paragraph plan for a description of your home or neighbourhood.

**a)** Decide what specific topic or thing you will describe in each paragraph and give it a title.

**b)** Then add the specific details about that topic or thing that you will describe in more detail.

1. **My street**

*Long and thin*

*Row of terrace houses on either side*

*All look the same – red bricks*

*Different coloured doors*

2. **My house**

*…*

> **Examiner comment**
>
> When you write to describe you can always add more details. If necessary you can invent details to make it more interesting.

## Language

**ACTIVITY 2**

Read this sentence from the description of the pit:

*Uneven rock walls rise several stories above my head.*

1 • What **adjectives** has the writer used to describe the walls?
   • What is the effect of including these adjectives? How would the text change without them?
   • What **verb** has the writer used to describe the walls?
   • What effect is created? What does it make you think about this place?

   Find:
   • three more interesting adjectives in the extract – explain why each one is effective.
   • three more interesting verbs in the extract – explain why each one is effective.

2 Look back at your plan for Activity 1. Write one paragraph, including a range of adjectives and verbs to make the description more vivid.

## Sentence structure

**ACTIVITY 3**

This is from paragraph 4 of the pit:

Repetition                                    List

People are everywhere, all dressed in black, all shouting and talking, expressive, gesturing. I don't see any elderly people in the crowd. Are there any old Dauntless?

Question

1 Notice the sentence structure that the writer has used.

   The writer begins with a long, **complex sentence**. Can you think of a reason why?

2 What is the effect of the question?

3 Choose another paragraph from the plan you produced. Write it, using a range of sentence structures to engage the reader.

Remember you can use complex sentences to add detail and short, simple sentences for impact or emphasis. For example:

*I struggled to think of how to describe him because he is such an unusual character, then it came to me. Rugged. He is rugged, and that says it all.*

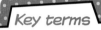

**Key terms**

**Adjective:** a describing word, it describes objects or places.

**Verbs:** a doing word; verbs are used to convey action.

**Key term**

**Complex sentence:** a sentence with one main clause and two or more subordinate clauses.

## How to produce a detailed plan

**Describe this scene.**

Begin by creating a spider diagram of initial ideas. Maybe identify the different elements you are going to describe.

Put your ideas into a list. Decide what the topic of each paragraph is going to be. You might start by describing the general scene and then focus on the tree and house in the middle. Alternatively, you could start by focusing on the house and then describe the scene in the background.

Decide on five paragraphs and give each one a 'heading' in your notes.

1 The spiral staircase

2 The trees in the background

3 The big tree at the front

4 ....

5 .....

Make some notes under each heading. Find some interesting adjectives and verbs you might use. Can you also jot down some effective repetition, a list and a rhetorical question?

1 The spiral staircase

winding upwards, snaking round the trunk like a curled ribbon, leading to the perched playhouse, camouflaged to blend with the wood

Boost your grade

This is a plan produced by a Grade 3 student, about to describe the best teacher they have ever had.

> Para 1: where he worked and what he did
>
> Para 2: what he looked like
>
> Para 3: where I met him and what he taught me for
>
> Para 4: how he behaved and taught
>
> Para 5: what people thought about him
>
> Para 6: why I liked him so much

This is a logical plan. However, it is clearly lacking in detail.

Develop the plan so that it looks more likely to lead to a Grade 5. If you wish, you can focus on an excellent teacher you have known.

Add the details you might put in each paragraph that are likely to lift your grade.

## 2 Adding more description of place

You can enhance your descriptions still further – and some techniques are particularly suited to descriptive writing:

- similes
- metaphors
- the use of the senses
- personification
- emotive words.

## Practising for success

When you are writing descriptions of places and scenes, you need to make the reader feel as if they are actually in that place.

### ACTIVITY 1

Read this description of a football stadium, written by a Grade 2 student.

> The pitch was green and the white lines stood out. The crowd were all shouting. We started to sing and swear and point at the away supporters. Then the teams came out.

This describes what is happening, but adds no vivid descriptive touches.

**1** Discuss why this student response is better.

> There is nothing like a football stadium at night when the floodlights are on. The pitch is like a green carpet and the reds, whites and blues shine. The voice of the announcer echoes around, with the music booming louder too. Your bottle of coke tastes wonderful; you smell the gum and the pies around you. You can look across at the opposition fans, jumping in waves of colour. Then our anthem begins and two lines of men walk out and the clapping explodes and it is as if life is about to begin again.
>
> (Grade 5)

**2** Identify:

- similes
- metaphors
- the use of **senses**.

Here is the same Grade 2 student describing a shopping centre:

> There are people everywhere. They push to get through and their kids are dragged with them. Inside, the shops are heaving. Some women spend ages picking things up and putting them down again. And not buying them. If their husbands are with them, they look bored. But they never help with the kids.

**3** How might this be improved? Add ideas to a table like the one below, putting in similes, metaphors and additions relating to the senses when you can:

| DETAIL | ADDITION |
|---|---|
| People everywhere | Simile: swarming like bees |
| | Metaphor: deranged people |
| | Senses: smelling sweaty/smelling of smoke/babies screaming |
| | |
| | |

**The senses:** feeling, taste, touch, what you hear and smell.

Examiner comment

Practising the use of similes and metaphors in particular can pay huge dividends. They always make your writing seem more imaginative – but try to avoid **clichés** if you can.

Key term

**Cliché:** something we have heard many times before.

**Key terms**

**Personification:** giving something that is not human the characteristics of a person, e.g. the wind screamed angrily.

**Emotive words:** words that describe an emotion or feeling, or make the reader feel a certain way.

{ **nigh** means 'nearly'

**not favourable** means something is bad }

Now, read this extract. It is taken from 'South: the endurance expedition' by Sir Ernest Shackleton. This book tells the true story of a dangerous journey by ship to the icy Antarctic, in 1914.

The writer has used **personification** and **emotive words** to describe the sea during a bad storm.

This personification not only makes the rocks seems alive but it makes it seem like they want to eat the boat. It helps us to imagine what it would have felt like on that ship and how scared the men must have felt.

Here and there the hungry rocks were close to the surface, and over them the great waves broke, swirling viciously and spouting thirty and forty feet into the air. The rocky coast appeared to descend sheer to the sea. Our need of water and rest was **well nigh** desperate, but to have attempted a landing at that time would have been suicidal. Night was drawing near, and the weather indications were **not favourable**.

These emotive words make the sea seem very dangerous and create a tense atmosphere

Sir Ernest Shackleton, *South: the endurance expedition* (1999)

**4 a)** Use this photo to help you write a description of the sky during a bad storm. What atmosphere do you want to create?

**b)** Include some emotive words and personification to enhance your description.

**5** Read the responses from these two students. Which one do you think is most effective, and why?

## Student A

> The lightning shot down from the sky. It lit up the sky around it. The sky looked blue and silver. There were lots of different lightning bolts in the sky and the clouds were a dark purple colour.

## Student B

> The sky angrily fired down a handful of lightning bolts like arrows from a huge bow. The wind howled miserably and the thunder angrily murmured in the background. The clouds began to cry big wet tears that soaked the ground below.

**6** Find an example of:
- a simile
- personification
- emotive words.

**7** Write a paragraph describing a snowfall.

Include as many of the following techniques as you can:
- simile
- metaphor
- use of the senses
- personification
- emotive language.

When you have finished, underline and label the techniques you have used.

## Moving from the general to the specific

When describing a place, writers will often move from describing the general scene to something more **specific** within it.

{ **specific** details are precise details }

For example:

A generalised paragraph about what the Lake District is like, then paragraphs on Windermere, Coniston… and so on

Or:

A generalised opening to a paragraph, followed by details which clarify the first statement or statements.

## ACTIVITY 2

Look at the photograph below.

**1** How might you describe it, in general terms? What major items would you write about in each paragraph that follows?

What is the general point you would make in each of your paragraph openings?

Then, what details would you add within the paragraphs?

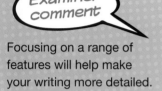

**Examiner comment**

Focusing on a range of features will help make your writing more detailed. Describing even the smallest thing will help your reader picture things more clearly.

**Boost your grade**

Read this student's description of the big wheel based on the picture above:

> In the distance, there was what at first appeared to be an impressive big wheel. However, when you got closer, it was rickety and old. It swayed gently from side to side like a tree in the breeze. Rusty spokes spiked out from the small centre and appeared to be holding the whole thing together. I wasn't so sure! At the end of each spoke dangled a carriage. Each one had been painted in bright primary colours but the paint was now peeling. A bright yellow fence surrounded the whole thing. I suppose it was supposed to be welcoming but to me it just screamed 'Danger! Stay away!' The whole thing looked like it could collapse at any minute; there was no way I was going anywhere near it!

- This student would be awarded a high Grade 5 for this writing because she has developed from her topic sentence:
- She has used a wide range of effective vocabulary – including adjectives and verbs.
- She has used the linguistic devices simile and personification.
- She has used a range of sentence structures and types that have been well controlled. Compound sentences add detail, and short simple sentences add impact and emphasis.
- She has used punctuation accurately including exclamation marks to emphasise some strong emotions.

Write your own paragraph about something else in the picture. Aim for Grade 5 standard.

# 3 Describing people

In this section you will learn how to use a range of techniques to describe a person, including adding direct speech. You will also think about how to structure a description of a person.

## Practising for success

Read this extract from *A Christmas Carol* by Charles Dickens. It is describing the character Scrooge.

Oh! But he was a tight-fisted hand at the grindstone, Scrooge! A squeezing, wrenching, grasping, scraping, clutching, **covetous** old sinner! Hard and sharp as flint…secret, and self-contained, and **solitary** as an oyster. The cold within him froze his old features, nipped his pointed nose, shrivelled his cheek, stiffened his **gait**; made his eyes red, his thin lips blue; and spoke out **shrewdly** in his grating voice. A frosty **rime** was on his head, and on his eyebrows, and his wiry chin. He carried his own low temperature always about with him; he iced his office in the **dog-days**; and didn't thaw it one degree at Christmas.

   External heat and cold had little influence on Scrooge. No warmth could warm, no wintry weather chill him. No wind that blew was bitterer than he, no falling snow was more intent upon its purpose, no pelting rain less open to **entreaty**.

Charles Dickens, *A Christmas Carol* (1843)

The writer uses many cold details to describe Scrooge.

What does this make you think that he might be like as a person? (What are the **connotations**?)

**covetous** means greedy

**solitary** means alone, unsociable

**gait** is 'walk'

**shrewdly** means sharply

**rime** is ice

**dog-days** are hottest days

**entreaty** is a request (e.g. to stop)

---

> ### Key terms
>
> **Connotation:** the feeling or idea you get from a word (not its literal meaning).
>
> *The word 'red' has connotations of love, danger and heat.*

## ACTIVITY 1

**1** In this passage Dickens describes Scrooge's appearance and also tells us what his personality is like. Find some words and phrases that describes:

   **a)** his appearance     **b)** his personality.

**2** The writer uses different language techniques to describe Scrooge. Find an example of each of the following:

- adjectives
- verbs
- similes
- metaphors
- exaggeration.

**3** The writer also uses some interesting sentence techniques to enhance the description. Find an example of each of the following:

- short simple sentences for emphasis or impact
- long, complex sentences to add detail
- **exclamations**
- lists
- repetition.

Notice how all of these techniques work together to create a very negative impression of this person.

**4** Think about a person you admire – it might be a member of your family, a friend, a celebrity or a character from a film or TV programme.

   **a)** Decide what main impression you want to create of this person – do you want to show that they are friendly, brave, strong, funny, scary?

   **b)** Plan a description of this person. Remember to think about their personality, as well as their appearance, their history, stories about them and how others see them. Think about how you admire them in general terms too.

**Key term**

**Exclamation:** remark expressing strong emotion. Exclamations can be used to show anger, surprise or joy.

### Using direct speech to develop a description of a person

Writers often use direct speech to develop their description of a person. Through speech you can show not only *what* a person says, but also *how* they say it.

## ACTIVITY 2

Read this short passage of speech.

> However, it was when the stranger spoke that I felt most **scared**. He boomed, 'Alright kid? Is your mum or dad home?'
>
> 'No,' I **squeaked**, wishing they were.
>
> 'No worries kid!' he bellowed, 'I'll just come back later. You tell him Big Pete was here! They'll know what it's about.' Then he was gone. I **slammed the door quickly** and breathed a **sigh of relief**.

Notice how another character – the narrator – has been used to improve the description of this person. This character's reactions (in bold) to the person emphasise how intimidating he is.

1 Find and record all the words and phrases that show us how this person speaks.

2 How does the speech help to create an impression of Big Pete?

3 Think again about the person you were planning to describe in Activity 1. Write a section of your description, using speech to bring it to life.

When describing people, it is vital that you plan carefully, so that you produce a description, not a story. Consider this title:

**Write a description of someone you met only once or twice but who made a big impression on you – either good or bad.**

Produce a detailed plan, making sure you:

● divide your plan into sensible sections    ● focus on the title.

And include the:

● similes    ● adjectives

● metaphors    ● exaggeration

you intend to use.

Also, indicate where you will use direct speech and what it will show.

## 4 Writing to describe an occasion

In your exam, you may be asked to describe an occasion. To do this, you will need to describe the place and possibly some of the people, but also the action.

## Practising for success

Read this opening description of an occasion: a school leavers party.

> The once dull walls of the school gym were now decorated with balloons, streamers and posters — from floor to ceiling. Incredibly, the balloons were yellow and brown (our school colours). I've never seen brown balloons before! You'd think they'd look horrid but strangely they really helped to brighten the whole place up. The streamers were different shades of yellow — pale lemon through to glittering gold — and they all fluttered in the breeze that was blowing through the open windows. Giant posters screamed out the words: Happy Leavers Night Class of 2014!

**Examiner comment**

You can also use speech in a description of a place: snippets of what people say can help develop the atmosphere. For example:

*'Wow!' she said.*

*'Can you believe anywhere could be so bleak?' he asked.*

**Examiner comment**

In this case, you might be writing a story of a kind (e.g. if you are describing what happened at a wedding reception or on a trip). However, remember that the descriptive details are still the vital elements.

A **connective** phrase is used to link and sequence the ideas in the two paragraphs. This phrase helps to guide the reader through the occasion being described.

> In the middle of all the excitement, I spotted our Headteacher on the stage at the back of the room. He was pacing about like a caged lion, nervously twiddling the piece of paper in his hand but he actually looked really proud. He was wearing a smart black suit and a bow tie and was smiling down at us as we chatted noisily to one another and looked admiringly around the room.

### Key term

**Connective:** words or phrases which link and sequence ideas in sentences, paragraphs and whole texts. Connectives of time (e.g. before, after, later on, suddenly), place (e.g. amidst, above, in the distance) and result (e.g. because of this, as a result, consequently) will be useful when writing to describe.

### Examiner comment

Consider adding connectives to your plan, to help you move between paragraphs when you come to write a response.

Notice how the opening paragraph gives a general overview of the scene. The next paragraph then describes something specific in this scene – in this case, a person.

## ACTIVITY 1

**1** You will notice that a range of descriptive devices and sentence structures have been used here.

What techniques and structures can you see? Give an example of each one. For example:

*personification – posters **screamed** out*

The following paragraphs might describe what happened next.

You might need to describe other people who proved important, or the scenes which resulted.

**2** Consider this example exam writing task.

*You decide to enter this creative writing competition in your favourite music magazine.*

**Write a description of the last music gig you went to. We want to hear all about it!**

*You can invent any details you need.*

Produce a detailed plan, including all the techniques you know will get you a better grade.

 **Boost your grade** ↗

Read this student's response to the writing task in Question 2.

> I went to the LeedsFest this year. There were loads of bands there. In fact, I can't remember them all. The festival was in a big field and there were loads of people there and it was noisy and busy. The first band that we saw had a singer who was wearing these really strange clothes – all bright colours – and he looked a bit like a clown. This singer shouted 'OK everybody lets hear you' into the mic before he sang the first song and everybody started cheering. I didn't though because I didn't know who he was! After that we went and got some food I had a burger it was nice but it cost six pounds….

This student would be awarded a Grade 3. Think about how he could improve the response to get a better grade.

**a)** The vocabulary he has used is quite simple and sometimes repetitive. Find three words he could change to improve his vocabulary and description.

**b)** He has used a lot of compound sentences with the simple connective 'and'. Rewrite the first two sentences to add more variety to his sentence structure.

**c)** His sentences are not always marked accurately with punctuation. Rewrite the section with the direct speech so that it is punctuated accurately and has more impact.

**d)** His writing has not been organised into paragraphs. Find where new paragraphs are needed. What further details might he include in each paragraph to develop them further?

**e)** His writing is recounting an event; but what other things might he add to develop the writing?

**f)** List some similes and metaphors that he could have used to impress the examiner.

## Test yourself

Plan and write a description of an outing you have been on.

Remember to describe:

- the place
- the people
- what happened.

Make sure you include the descriptive techniques you have learnt about in this unit.

**What you have learned** !

In this unit you have learned how to:

- write to describe places, people and occasions
- organise your writing
- include a range of vocabulary
- gain extra marks by using descriptive techniques.

# Writing to narrate

**What this unit involves**

In this unit you will learn about:
⇨ planning your story
⇨ openings – how to begin your story
⇨ writing key passages in the story
⇨ endings
⇨ creating characters.

**What this unit involves**

This unit deals with Paper 1, Section B: Writing. You are likely to have an option to produce a piece of narrative writing, which will almost certainly be a short story or the beginning of a story.

You will have 45 minutes to do this: 40 marks are available.

These are some types of narrative task that you may get in the exam:

Write a story:
- with the title 'A Friend in Need'
- starting with the line 'The room was not at all as he/she/they had expected.'
- ending with the line 'In a few minutes it had sunk, leaving the waters lapping around the place where it had been.'
- about a place where rapid change takes place
- on the theme of love and hate.

## 1 Planning a short story

**Examiner comment**

Even if you are asked to write the opening section of a novel, you will have time to get quite a long way in – maybe the whole of the first chapter – so an effective structure is vital.

Spend a few minutes planning your story and you will avoid 'losing your way'.

A 'traditional' story is likely to:
- establish a *situation*
- introduce a *trigger* which sparks off the main events
- have some *challenge or conflict* – which will be closely connected to the trigger
- gradually become more exciting
- move to a *resolution* which deals with the problem – though this does not have to be a happy ending.

# Practising for success

## Planning

### ACTIVITY 1

Consider this task.

**Write a story that begins: 'The relationship started so well.'**

1 Decide who the story is going to be about – jot down brief notes about the characters.
2 Produce your spider diagram of ideas, suggesting what might happen. For example:

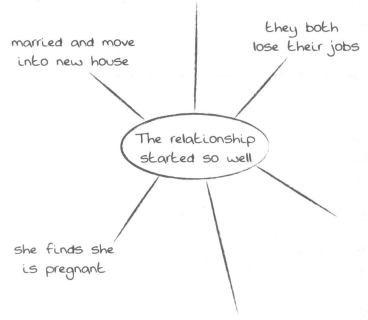

married and move into new house

they both lose their jobs

The relationship started so well

she finds she is pregnant

**Examiner comment**

You will have only about 35 minutes to actually write your story, after you have planned it, and allowing time for checking at the end. Therefore, try to limit yourself to just two or three main characters, who you can deal with in detail.

In a short story you do not have time to write about happening after happening, or scene after scene. Try to focus on just one or two major scenes – you can explain what has happened elsewhere by what people say.

For example, this is how a Grade 5 student presented a good deal of information very rapidly:

> When he walked through the door, his face was like thunder. 'I can't believe it,' he said. She looked frightened. 'I've been fired!' he said. 'How will we pay the mortgage?'
>
> She suddenly burst into tears. 'This can't be happening…' She held out a letter. 'Look what's just come for me…'

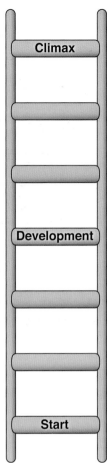

Climax

Development

Start

**3** Put your ideas into a logical order, moving from start to finish.

**4** Add details under each subheading, saying what you will include in that section.

Your story cannot be full of excitement from start to finish. Ideally, the tension will build steadily, so that you build to a climax.

You might then have a paragraph or two to 'tidy up' loose ends, or conclude. For example:

> It seemed to be all over. Finally, there was a chance for them to be happy. He took her in his arms and...

## Viewpoint and tense

You will also need to decide on what *tense* to write in and what *viewpoint* to use and then stick to them.

It is always safest to write as if everything happened in the past. It is hard to write in the present tense.

### ACTIVITY 2

Read this extract.

> Shabnam's face turns pale as she reads the letter. Then she crumples it up, before changing her mind and smoothing it out on the table. She gazes out of the window, her hand trembling violently, then tries to stand up, and fails. She walked to the door, put on her coat and stepped out into the morning.

**1** It reads like a Grade 5 to begin, but what goes wrong?

When thinking about viewpoint, you will have to decide whether to write in the first person (using *I* and *we*) or in the third person (*he, she, they*).

**A first-person narrative** is likely to make us feel particular sympathy for the **narrator**, but we can only see through his or her eyes:

> I looked across the bus and he was still sitting there. I couldn't decide what to do. Should I get off and run home from here? Or should I get off at my usual stop and know he would be right behind me as I made my way up the road...

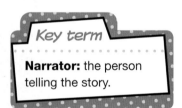

**Key term**

**Narrator:** the person telling the story.

A **third-person narrative** can focus on just one person in a similar way:

> She looked across the bus and he was still sitting there. She couldn't decide what to do. Should she…

Or, the narrator can be **omniscient** and aware of everyone's feelings and actions.

> She looked across the bus and was terrified when she saw him sitting there. He just wanted to be her friend – no more than that – but how could she know? As it was, she had a simple decision to make: should she get off the bus early and run the rest of the way? Or should she risk getting off at her normal stop? He didn't know what she was thinking, only that she looked worried, and that upset him more than anything.

**Key term**

**Omniscient:** all-knowing.

1 Show you have got the idea of using tense and person effectively by re-writing this extract from a Grade 2 story so that both are consistent.

> Ollie goes to the phone and picked it up. 'Hello?' he said, nervously. He thinks he knows the voice from somewhere.
>
> 'Listen to me carefully if you want your daughter back,' says the voice.
>
> I listened, and write down the address he gave me. It is somewhere on the other side of town – a place I didn't really know.

2 Which viewpoint and tense do you think would be best for the story you have planned, and why?

## 2 Openings – how to begin

### Who, what, where, when?

The opening of your story needs to do several things:

- get the reader's attention
- arouse the reader's curiosity about what will happen next
- provide basic information about the characters and what is going on
- set the scene – where and when the story starts.

# Practising for success

**When**

Read this story opening:

**What the characters are doing**

**Where they are**

Introduces first character, hinting at his relationship with the others through dialogue

Next character

Having a drink is 'the thing to do' in this situation (we wonder why)

{ **gimlet** is an alcoholic drink with gin, lime juice and soda

**mess boy** is a kitchen servant }

> It was now lunch-time and they were all sitting under the double green fly of the dining-tent pretending that nothing had happened.
>
> 'Will you have lime juice or lemon squash?' Macomber asked.
>
> 'I'll have a **gimlet**,' Robert Wilson told him.
>
> 'I'll have a gimlet too. I need something,' Macomber's wife said.
>
> 'I suppose it's the thing to do,' Macomber agreed. 'Tell him to make three gimlets.'
>
> The **mess boy** had started them already, lifting the bottles out of the canvas bags that sweated wet in the wind that blew through the trees that shaded the tents.
>
> Ernest Hemingway, *The Short Happy Life of Francis Macomber* (1936)

Raises a big question

Third character introduced, raising a question: why does she 'need' alcohol?

More scene-setting: what sort of place is this?

## ACTIVITY 1

1 Discuss how this opening raises questions, introduces the characters, and sets the scene.

2 Write the opening of a story in which something bad or awkward has just happened involving three characters. Before you begin, decide what has happened, and how each was involved.

In a short story, an effective way to set the scene quickly is to insert a few well-chosen details into the action, for example:

> It seemed a long walk across the marbled reception area of the Palace Hotel...
>
> The sand was in her hair, the screaming of the children was in her ears and the Bank Holiday sun beat down on the beach...

3 Use some of the techniques in the opening above to:
- find a way to suggest what time it is
- include some dialogue which introduces each character
- hint at what has happened
- include a few details to tell the reader where your characters are.

Discussion point

**4** Swap your opening with a partner. Give them feedback on whether they have successfully raised questions, introduced the characters, and set the scene.

## Other ways to get the reader's attention

You could get the reader's attention in other ways. For example:

- go straight into some action or dialogue
- present a strange statement from the narrator
- give some surprising information
- give a brief description of an unusual scene.

## ACTIVITY 2

**1** Read the following openings, and discuss how each one gets our attention.

### Source A

```
'Hotel des Pins!' said Harry. 'More like Hotel des Boobs.'
'Come away from that window,' said Brenda. 'Stop behaving
like a Peeping Tom.'
```
David Lodge, *Hotel des Boobs* (1986)

### Source B

Yesterday afternoon the six o'clock bus ran over Miss Bobbit.

Truman Capote, *Children on their Birthdays* (1949)

### Source C

It was a hidden Broadway restaurant in the dead of night, and a brilliant and mysterious group of society people, diplomats and members of the underworld were there.

F. Scott Fitzgerald, *Basil: The Freshest Boy* (1928)

**2** Copy the technique of one of these openings to write an opening to grab your reader's attention. Write one or two sentences. Here are some ideas to get you started:

- a shocking sound suggests an emergency
- someone is creeping through a jungle – day or night
- a waiter or waitress in a restaurant does something awful
- a frightening person shouts an order
- an unusual person introduces themself.

Below are two openings to stories written in response to this title:
**'Write a story about someone achieving an ambition.'**

**1** One opening is a Grade 5, the other a Grade 3. Decide which is which, and why one is so much better.

## Student A

> Dan was an ordinary sort of man who lived in a northern town. He used to live in London but he could not get a job there, so he had come back to his home town. One day he was talking to his friend Chris about football. They both wanted to play for their team but they did not think they had much chance.

## Student B

> It was now or never. Another minute and the last train would come thundering into the station. The rails already seemed to tremble in the moonlight.
>
> 'Er, excuse me,' he said, nervously.
>
> The pretty, dark-haired girl in the blue coat turned to look at him. 'Yes? Do I know you?' she said.

The better opening communicates ideas clearly. Vocabulary is chosen to create effects and the details and speech begin to reveal the characters and the setting. The sentence lengths and types are varied to interest the reader.

**2** Rewrite the Grade 3 answer – or part of it – improving it to Grade 5 standard.

## 3 Writing key passages in the story

Pay special attention to writing the key parts of your story, especially:

- the 'trigger moment' which sparks off the rest of the story
- any section making it clear what the 'stakes' are for the main character – what they have to gain or lose, which will be what 'hooks' the reader
- the climax.

Read the following two extracts on page 167 from later in the story quoted earlier in the unit (*The Short Happy Life of Francis Macomber*). They are told as flashbacks, explaining the awkward mood at the start of the story.

### ACTIVITY 1

**1** Answer the questions in the annotations on page 167.

### Extract A

Macomber is on a hunting holiday in Africa. He has wounded a lion. It is now his responsibility to kill it. He is afraid. The lion is in hiding, preparing to charge.

Kongoni, the old gun-bearer, in the lead watching the blood **spoor**, Wilson watching the grass for any movement, his big gun ready, the second gun-bearer looking ahead and listening, Macomber close to Wilson, his rifle cocked. They had just moved into the grass when Macomber heard the blood-choked coughing grunt, and saw the swishing rush in the grass. The next thing he knew he was running; running wildly, in panic in the open, running toward the stream.

**spoor** is a trail (of blood)

What is the mood here and what is it suggesting is about to happen?

The trigger incident: what does it tell us about Macomber?

## Extract B

When Macomber ran away, the expert hunter Wilson shot the lion at close range. This is what happened back in their vehicle.

What does this tell us about Macomber?

Once, he had reached over and taken his wife's hand without looking at her and she had removed her hand from his. Looking across the stream to where the gun-bearers were skinning out the lion he could see that she had been able to see the whole thing. While they sat there his wife had reached forward and put her hand on Wilson's shoulder. He turned and she had leaned forward over the low seat and kissed him on the mouth.

What has the event probably made his wife think about Macomber?

The stakes are high: Macomber will have to make up for his cowardice or lose his wife to Wilson

**2** Write two sections for a story in which the main character does something they regret.

- The first should show the trigger, making its importance clear.
- The second should show the stakes – what the main character stands to win or lose.

Here are some possible triggers:
- someone sends an email to the wrong person
- someone boasts about a skill they do not really have
- someone loses money they really needed, or a valued object (someone else's?)
- someone agrees to go on a date, then regrets it.

Here is part of a Grade 4 response to this task, in which the candidate includes the 'trigger moment'.

Some variety in sentence lengths

Overall, not exciting or engaging – and this is an important moment in the story

Her grandad was going to be 70 tomorrow and she had nothing to give him. Once she would have drawn him a picture and sprinkled glitter on it. But she knew that she was rubbish at drawing. Her eyes went over to the shelf with whisky on it. She saw a bottle that said 'Barrisdale Single Malt'. He liked to drink that, so she looked around and no one was looking and her parka had deep pockets so she put it into one of them.

Sensibly sequenced

Some suitable vocabulary

**3** Write a new, improved version of the paragraph.

## Writing the climax

The climax of a story will come towards the end, or even right at the end. One technique is to use sentence length to build your story towards a climax, as in the passage below, in which Macomber, who ran away from a lion, now shows courage by facing a buffalo.

Brief simile conveys urgent speed

Short descriptive phrases develop a fast rhythm

Short simile brings Macomber's experience to life without slowing us down

Repeated 'and', with close details, brings to final climax

Highly dramatic language

'He's dead in there,' Wilson said. 'Good work,' and he turned to grip Macomber's hand and as they shook hands, grinning at each other, the gun-bearer shouted wildly and they saw him coming out of the bush sideways, fast as a crab, and the buffalo coming, nose out, mouth tight closed, blood dripping, massive head straight out, coming in a charge, his little pig eyes bloodshot as he looked at them. Wilson, who was ahead, was kneeling shooting, and Macomber, as he fired, unhearing his shot in the roaring of Wilson's gun, saw fragments like slate burst from the huge boss of the horns, and the head jerked; he shot again at the wide nostrils and saw the horns jolt again and fragments fly, and he did not see Wilson now and, aiming carefully, shot again with the buffalo's huge bulk almost on him and his rifle almost level with the oncoming head, nose out, and he could see the little wicked eyes and the head started to lower and he felt a sudden white-hot, blinding flash explode inside his head and that was all he ever felt.

Ernest Hemingway, *The Short Happy Life of Francis Macomber* (1936)

## ACTIVITY 2

1 Obviously, you are unlikely to use sentences as long as these, but write a paragraph from a story in which someone is either:

**a)** confronting something frightening

or

**b)** trying to escape from it.

Discussion point

2 Swap paragraphs with a partner. See if your partner could have used any of the following techniques to improve their paragraph:

- a short simile
- a well-chosen detail
- a touch of speech
- dramatic descriptive language.

## Endings

If you have been asked to just write the start of a story, end it at a point where the reader will really want to know more. For example, this could be when the main character has started to rise to the central challenge, but we do not yet know if the plan will work.

If you are writing a whole story, it is usual to leave the reader feeling that it is complete: it should not just come to a sudden halt or fizzle out.

The only alternative might be if you want to finish with a 'cliff-hanger' so the reader is left to decide what might happen next. For example:

> *This seemed to be the end. But should they risk diving into the icy water a hundred metres below, or simply stand together as the wave of heat rushed towards them?*

Here are some possible types of ending:
- The main character overcomes their problem, or rises to their challenge.
- The beginning of the story is echoed, creating a comparison – then and now.
- A final incident shows what the main character has learned.
- A celebration, such as a wedding, prize-giving or party.
- There is a twist – something unexpected is revealed at the last moment.

In this story, an elderly couple are given a monkey's paw which is said to grant three wishes. The old man wishes for £200 – which the couple receive in compensation when their son is killed by being fatally mangled by machinery. The old woman makes the next wish – to have their son alive again. They hear a knocking at their door and the woman rushes down.

Read the ending and notice the annotations showing how it works as an ending:

*Verb and adverb suggest he is desperate*

*Creates suspense and sense of fear – what is 'the thing'?*

*Sudden dramatic change with new paragraph: tension collapses*

*Dramatic language builds to a climax*

*Tension and suspense*

*Reveals that 'the thing' has gone; peace now returns*

*Wife shows her feelings*

'The bolt,' she cried, loudly. 'Come down. I can't reach it.'

But her husband was on his hands and knees groping wildly on the floor in search of the paw. If he could only find it before the thing outside got in. A perfect fusillade of knocks reverberated through the house, and he heard the scraping of a chair as his wife put it down in the passage against the door. He heard the creaking of the bolt as it came slowly back, and at the same moment he found the monkey's paw, and frantically breathed his third and last wish.

The knocking ceased suddenly, although the echoes of it were still in the house. He heard the chair drawn back, and the door opened. A cold wind rushed up the staircase, and a long loud wail of disappointment and misery from his wife gave him courage to run down to her side, and then to the gate beyond. The street lamp flickering opposite shone on a quiet and deserted road.

W. W. Jacobs, *The Monkey's Paw* (1902)

## ACTIVITY 3

1 Discuss what you think the old man's wish was, and why he made it.

2 This story has a *moral* – a lesson to be learned from it. Discuss what you think the moral could be. For example, could it be one of the following:

- be careful what you wish for?
- fate is unavoidable?
- don't try to cheat death?
- steer clear of magic?

3 Write the final two or three paragraphs of a story with a moral. Choose from:

- Honesty is the best policy.
- Money can't buy happiness.
- Love will find a way.
- Patience pays off in the end.

Choose your language to create tension and suspense, building to a climax, like the ending of *The Monkey's Paw*.

Decide on a story, the two characters involved and the setting.

Your ending should have a climax, then show what happens afterwards.

 Here is the ending of a Grade 5 story written in response to the exam task 'Write a story entitled "Revenge is sweet".'

The white-coated Evans led Barford across the high metal walkway, glancing back occasionally.

'I think I ought to be getting back,' said the manager. 'My wife will be wondering where I am. Women are always worrying!'

'Yes, of course,' said Evans, 'but you haven't seen the best of it yet. Trust me. Just a little further. After you. Emily won't miss you, I'm sure.'

'How did you know –?' Barford began.

As they passed beneath an overhead light, the manager suddenly swung round to face Evans. 'Wait a minute. Don't I recognise you?' Evans nodded.

There was no guard rail and it took only the slightest push for Tom Evans to tip his rival over the edge. Barford's high-pitched scream was lost in the bubbling vat of toffee into which he fell, fifty feet below.

1 Find where the ending uses:
- interesting and expressive vocabulary
- effective adjectives
- varied sentences.

2 Even from this extract, what do you know about:
- the scene
- the men
- the story?

3 Now write an ending of your own in response to the same task. Use:
- conversation
- touches of detail to set the scene
- enough detail to let us know who the characters are and perhaps what they are like.

# 4 Creating characters

## Show, don't tell

You will develop your two or three main characters as your story develops. It is better to get straight into the action than to spend a long time at the beginning just telling the reader what your characters are like.

The main ways to show what a character is like are:
- what they do
- what they say
- how others respond to them.

# Practising for success

## Presenting a character

Read the following extracts from student stories written in response to the task 'Write a story with the title "Pride comes before a fall".'

## Source A

> Donna was the kind of girl who was never wrong. She thought she was pretty clever, and she just couldn't stand the thought that she'd made a mistake. She was also very stuck up, always thinking she was the most attractive girl in the class and that all the boys were after her. As a result, other girls tended not to like her very much, but she didn't really care.
>
> (Grade 3)

## Source B

> Damian swaggered in, his bag hung casually over his shoulder, giving Debbie his 'special' smile at he passed and firing an imaginary gun at her. She gazed up at him starry-eyed.
>
> 'All right, Debs? Catch you later, eh.'
>
> Laid back in his chair, he took out his i-Phone, and scrolled down, muttering:
>
> 'Nah, nah ... maybe ... if I can be bovvered ... no way.'
>
> He made sure everyone could see it was the latest model.
>
> (Grade 5)

### ACTIVITY 1

1 Decide why the second extract is more effective in revealing character in an interesting way. Explain your opinion.
2 Bearing in mind how effective the second extract is, write the opening to a story with the same title. Introduce a main character, *showing* the reader what they are like.

## Relationships, conflicts, and what characters want

Remember that a story needs a problem or challenge. One type of problem or challenge is a character clash. Characters come into conflict because they want different things.

ACTIVITY 2

**1** Read the following passage and discuss:
- What do the characters want?
- How do we know?
- What action could develop from this?

McMurphy, a mental hospital inmate, wants to watch a baseball match on TV. The head nurse refuses permission, so he goes and sits in front of the blank TV screen.

> *What does his body language show? (What does he* want *it to show?)*

> *Why do you think she hesitates?*

> *What does this show?*

> *Simile shows her rising anger and tension*

> *buffer is a floor polisher*

> *Tension still mounting*

He sits that way, with his hands crossed behind his head and his feet stuck out in a chair, a smoking cigarette sticking out from under his hatbrim – watching the TV screen.

The nurse stands this as long as she can; then she comes to the door of the Nurses' Station and calls across to him he'd better help the men with the housework. He ignores her.

'I said, Mr McMurphy, that you are supposed to be working during these hours.' Her voice has a tight whine like an electric saw ripping through pine. 'Mr McMurphy, I'm *warning* you!'

Everybody's stopped what he was doing. She looks around her, then takes a step out of the Nurses' Station towards McMurphy.

'You're committed, you realize. You are ... under the jurisdiction of me ... the staff.' She's holding up a fist, all those red-orange fingernails burning into her palm. 'Under jurisdiction and control–'

Harding shuts off the **buffer**, and leaves it in the hall, and goes pulls him a chair up alongside McMurphy and sits down and lights him a cigarette too.

'Mr Harding! You return to your scheduled duties!'

I think how her voice sounds like it hit a nail, and this strikes me so funny I almost laugh.

'Mr Har-*ding*!'

Then Cheswick goes and gets him a chair, and then Billy Bibbit goes, and then Scanlon and then Fredrickson and Sefelt, and then we all put down our mops and brooms and scouring rags and we all go pull us chairs up.

'You men – Stop this. Stop!'

Ken Kesey, *One Flew Over the Cuckoo's Nest* (1973)

**2** How in control is she now?

**3** Write about thirty lines of your own in which one character wants one or more other characters to do something that they refuse to do. Choose words to show mounting frustration and tension.

**Boost your Grade** Remember that you will have to choose a viewpoint and stick to it: first person ('I') or third person ('he', 'she'). If you choose to tell your story in the first person, you can reveal the narrator's character by how they tell the story.

Read the following first-person narrative. Study the annotations.

Recreates narrator's experience

Shows she felt jealous of her parents

Mummy and papa were talking again, soft whispers, sss sss sss. My mother's bracelets jingled as she seemed to wipe something from her face. This was my birthday and they were leaving me out again. I squeezed my hot dog and suddenly the sausage shot into my mouth and lodged firmly in my windpipe. I was too shocked to move, my fingers curled uselessly into my fists. They were still talking, engrossed, I could see papa's eyes in the mirror, darting from my mother's face to the unfolding road. I thought of writing SAUSAGE STUCK on the windscreen and then realised I could not spell sausage. I was going to die in the back of the car and somewhere inside me, I felt thrilled. It was so dramatic. This was by far the most exciting thing that had ever happened to me.

Makes herself a comic figure

Wants to feel important? Finds life dull?

Meera Syal, *Anita and Me* (1996)

The parents suddenly realise their child is choking. Tell the story of what happens next from one of their points of view. Try to reveal their character by how they tell the story.

## Test yourself

Write a story set in what is normally a quiet and sleepy village.

You should:

- plan thoroughly using the skills practised in this unit
- write an engaging opening and move to an effective ending
- use two or three characters and just two or three scenes.

**What you have learned** !

In this unit you have learned how to:

- plan your story
- write an effective story opening and different sorts of endings
- write key passages, including the trigger moment and climax
- create characters using action, dialogue and viewpoint.

# Writing with a viewpoint

**In this unit you will learn about:**

⇒ assessing the task
⇒ explaining your point of view
⇒ arguing a case
⇒ writing to persuade
⇒ using evidence.

## 1 Planning the response and explaining your viewpoint

### Purpose, audience and context

The writing task you are given will always have three key elements:

- **Purpose** – what the writing is supposed to do ('explain your views', 'argue' or 'persuade').
- **Audience** – the kind of readers you should aim at ('magazine readers', 'local business people', etc.).
- **Context** – the form of the writing ('a letter', 'an article' or 'a speech').

Here is an example of an exam writing task with the purpose, audience and context labelled:

Context            Purpose

*Write an article for your school magazine to persuade students to volunteer for a scheme to help elderly people in your community.*

Audience

## Practising for success

### ACTIVITY 1

1 Write down the important words or phrases in the following exam questions and label them P, A, C according to whether they show purpose, audience or context.

**A.** Write a letter to your school governors arguing either *for* or *against* their decision to sell off the school playing fields to a housing developer to raise money for the school.

**B.** Write a speech to be delivered to local business people to persuade them to sponsor a local competition to get young people interested in careers in the world of business.

**2** The following two tasks begin with a statement. Identify the most important words in the statement, but then look for the purpose, audience and context in the second part of the task.

**A.** *'Schools should not ask students to think about the meaning of life or how to be happy: they should just teach practical skills for the workplace.'*

Write an article for a broadsheet newspaper's weekly magazine explaining your views on this statement.

**B.** *'Holidays abroad are a waste of time and money. You can have a better time in Britain at half the cost.'*

This statement has appeared in your local paper. Write a letter to the editor explaining how far you agree, and why.

## Planning your response

Here is a typical task with the purpose, audience and context highlighted.

*Audience* – educated readers of serious papers like *The Times*, who appreciate ideas and interesting language

*Purpose* – 'explain', making it clear why you hold your views; don't give a list of arguments and evidence

> Write a *broadsheet newspaper magazine article explaining your views* on TV talent shows.

*Context* – magazine article: readers expect to be entertained as well as informed

## ACTIVITY 2

**1** On a new page, make a spider diagram of your ideas for this task. Focus on no more than three talent shows.

**2** List your ideas in an order that makes sense.

**3** Make brief notes beneath each main idea, to indicate what you will say in that section and your approaches, including, for example:

- one or two examples, such as key moments or contestants
- intelligent ideas on the subject, such as 'an inspiration for young people'
- any convincing and entertaining words or phrases that you think of – such as 'smug judges', 'jittery contestants too nervous to sing in tune', 'rags to riches', etc.
- rhetorical questions and repetition for effect
- how ideas can be linked.

**4** Write a rough final sentence summing up your ideas. This should serve as the target towards which your answer is heading.

> **Examiner comment**
>
> If you are asked to write a speech, keep it formal. However, you should make a special effort to appeal to the target audience, as in 'Intelligent viewers will realise ...'

## Explaining your point of view

When you begin writing, you need to make everything clear for the reader.

'Explaining' your point of view means:
- telling readers what your views on the subject are
- helping readers to understand why you hold these views.

### ACTIVITY 3

Read the following first half of an 'opinion' article. Look at the annotations to see how the author makes her views clear, justifies them, and entertains.

Notice how the opening paragraph 'sets the scene' and grabs the reader's attention

Engages reader with question

Makes viewpoint clear by negative language choice

Entertains with 'non-reasons' to build up to the real one

the Big Four refers to the top four supermarkets in the UK

euphemistically means using a word to make something seem less bad than it really is

How much, on a scale of one to ten, do you care that supermarkets are losing £200 million a year to 'grazers' — people who shop while stuffing their faces with food for which they have no intention of paying? I'm guessing that, essentially, you don't give a toss. **The Big Four** make umpteen billion pounds out of us every year, you think, they can cope with losing the odd, sweaty Scotch egg!

Well — and this amazes even *me* — I care. It's not that I'm sucking up to supermarket bosses because I might one day need a shelf-stacking job (well, maybe a bit — these are uncertain times), or even that I object to such shoppers **euphemistically** being termed 'grazers' when they are just grubbing shoplifters. No, it's that I know how pig-ignorant supermarket customers can be and I'd like to see them punished — preferably with an electric prod.

... I was a trainee manager for a supermarket for eight of the most miserable months of my life (on second thoughts, shove that shelf-stacking job) and have seen the transformation that takes place whenever people get behind a trolley. They go into a wild-eyed trance, apparently convinced that they're the most stressed and busy people in the world, tutting and sighing and stampeding the aisles in very bad moods. But in those days I had to be diplomatic about their beastliness, and now I don't.

Statistic shows that this issue is important

Uses second person to address reader, guessing what reader might think

Entertainingly shocking exaggeration of her real view

Explains why she knows about this subject

**176**

> I recall having to remain polite while being bawled out by a businessman for refusing to reduce a packet of best steak that I had watched him deliberately damage with his thumb; summoned by an outraged woman and ordered to place loose new potatoes in a plastic bag for her because they were 'covered in soil' (new potatoes — ya don't say?); called a 'snotty cow' for merely pointing out that a customer's money-off vouchers were for a different supermarket chain.
>
> Carol Midgley, *The Times* (2009)

Uses three lively anecdotes (true personal stories) to support her main point

**1** Imagine you find this task in the exam:

*Some shopkeepers say: 'The customer is always right.'*

*Explain your views on how customers are treated in shops.*

**a)** Think of, or make up, three **anecdotes** about your own experiences of shopping or shoppers that you could use in tackling this writing task.

**b)** Think of one main point you could make. Write a sentence expressing it.

**c)** Write a paragraph beginning with your main point and then backing it up with your three anecdotes.

**Key term**

**Anecdote**: a short, sometimes entertaining story from personal experience.

**Examiner comment**

Your views do not have to be totally one-sided. You could use phrases like 'Of course, some people say…', or 'We also have to remember that…' or 'On the other hand' (e.g. 'Most shop assistants are polite and helpful. On the other hand, some…')

Here is part of a Grade 2 response to the task on page 177. Read it, and the assessment of it that follows.

1 Discuss with a friend what, exactly, is wrong with it.
2 Rewrite it to achieve a higher grade. Keep the same information but change as much of the wording and punctuation as you think is necessary.

> I think shops dont treat teenagers especially right. They look at us suspicious like we was going to rob them or make a mess which most of us arent. I went into a shop and I wanted to take two pairs of jeans into a booth because I couldnt decide and the shop person said Oi – one item – can't you read. That was well out of order. There was a time I gave the girl a tenner and she swears blind it was five. I made her look in the till and I was right. She still didnt say sorry nor nothing. Some assistants is nice and helpful.

**Assessment comment**

This student communicates some ideas and backs them up with two anecdotes. However, the communication is not always completely clear and the choice of language is too informal. Some word choices could be more effective. There are many technical errors.

# 2 Arguing a case

If you are asked to 'argue', 'give your arguments' or 'justify your views', you will be expected to present reasons for your views in a logical order. This should lead the reader step by step to agreeing with you, or at least to understanding your views.

## Practising for success

### Putting forward your main arguments

ACTIVITY 1

1 Read the following Grade 5 opening of a student response to the task below, then study the annotations showing what makes it a Grade 5.

*Top sportspeople should be role models.*

Write an article for a broadsheet newspaper putting forward your arguments for or against this view.

Dramatic opening to engage reader

More interesting than 'bit': makes us picture it

An effective list of 3 – making three similar points, repeating 'letting ...down', ending in most important point

Gets in the key information in a few words

Topic sentence introducing paragraph and linked to previous one

Signals a logically linked argument

Effective linking of ideas

Second part of a balanced sentence making a key point

When millionaire footballer Luis Suarez sunk his teeth into the shoulder of Italian defender Giorgio Chiellini in the 2014 World Cup, he wasn't just letting himself down. He wasn't even just letting Uruguay down or his team Liverpool. He was letting down the thousands of young people who think of him as their hero. The same goes for cyclists who only win races because they have taken drugs, and world-class cricketers who get into punch-ups.

These people get paid huge sums of money. This is because their sporting ability makes money for their clubs and TV. However, this is only because people identify with them and therefore want them to do well. Young people, especially, see them and dream of being like them. We all need heroes to inspire us, but a hero who behaves badly or cheats is worse than no hero at all.

**2** Imagine that the student has several other points to make:

**a)** Cyclists are under pressure to use drugs to compete.
**b)** Some footballers cheat on their wives and girlfriends.
**c)** Fame brings responsibilities to fans.
**d)** Suarez has been guilty of three biting incidents.
**e)** No one is perfect, but celebrities should at least admit their mistakes.
**f)** Suarez pretended that the Italian player had attacked him.
**g)** Lance Armstrong won the Tour de France cycle race seven times but has now been stripped of his titles for drug-taking.

How would you order these points in the essay to run on logically from each other?

**3** Take one or more of the points listed above and use them to write a new paragraph developing the argument of the 'Top sportspeople should be role models' article. Link your ideas using words like these:

*however     despite     because     although     on the other hand     but*

Begin your paragraph with a topic sentence telling readers what the paragraph as a whole is about.

## Anticipating a counter-argument or viewpoint

A **counter-argument** is an opposing argument. In writing to argue, it is very effective to put forward a counter-argument so that you can dismiss it by showing its weaknesses compared with your own. This shows you have thought about other viewpoints and still believe in your own.

Here is an example of a counter-argument, from the Grade 5 student response to 'Top sportspeople should be role models':

> Of course there are some who say that a top sportsperson's commitment is to doing the best they can in their sport — not to being a role model. Why, they ask, should being good at football mean you have to be good at being faithful to your wife or girlfriend? But this attitude fails to accept that fame brings responsibilities. Sportspeople who try to shrug them off are letting down the fans who pay their sky-high wages.

## ACTIVITY 2

1 Look for examples of the following strengths in this response:
   a) a well-chosen phrase suggesting irresponsibility
   b) a rhetorical question (one asked for dramatic effect, not expecting an answer)
   c) a phrase introducing the counter-argument
   d) a verb suggesting that the counter-argument is inadequate
   e) an exaggerated but effective adjective
   f) a word signalling the start of the dismissal of the counter-argument.
2 Imagine the task is slightly different and you have written an article arguing that pop stars should be role models, and not behave badly. Write a paragraph like the one above presenting and dismissing a counter-argument.

   Your paragraph could begin:

   *But surely, you might think, pop stars are meant to behave badly ...*

## Reaching a conclusion

Your conclusion should draw your arguments together, briefly reminding readers of how you reached this point, and leaving them thinking they should agree with you. Do not just repeat yourself. Nor should you try to squeeze in a completely new argument or piece of evidence.

Two effective techniques are:
- refer back to the opening paragraph, showing that you knew where you were going all along
- refer back to the task by quoting a phrase from it.

**Examiner comment**

These features are sure to impress your examiner.

Read the conclusion to the Grade 5 student response to 'Top sportspeople should be role models' that you have looked at earlier in this unit:

Returns to opening topic, driving home why it is important

No-nonsense triple plan of action

Strong statement drawing together earlier points about responsibility

> Whether they like it or not, sporting celebrities have power. And they have a duty to use that power for good. So if Luis Suarez wants to make it up to his fans, he should admit that he has a problem, get help, and stop biting people. That would give us a real role model – a hero who's big enough to face up to his mistakes.

Statement logically connected to first (helped by repeating 'power'), leading into how celebrities should behave

Refers back to writing task; leaves reader with an important point to think about

ACTIVITY 3

1 Write a concluding paragraph to an article for a broadsheet newspaper arguing *either* that media celebrities *do* or *do not* have a duty to be good role models. Use some of the techniques in the Grade 5 response above.

**Boost your grade ⇗**

1 Swap your conclusion with another student. Annotate each other's conclusions in the way that the response above has been annotated, to show their strong points.
2 Reread your own conclusion. Could you improve it – for example by choosing more effective words, altering the **sentence** types or order, or referring more effectively to the topic?
3 Rewrite it, making the necessary improvements.

# 3 Persuading the reader to accept your views

Writing to persuade involves explaining your views, and putting forward logically connected arguments. However, it also puts a special emphasis on three things:

● the use of language techniques to influence your reader
● word choices that influences your reader's emotional response to your views
● getting your reader to agree with you – and sometimes to act on that belief.

You are likely to use **emotive language** – chosen to produce an emotional response in the reader or listener. Certain word choices can influence the reader to see something in a positive or negative way through their emotional appeal.

## Practising for success

### ACTIVITY 1

Read this example of emotive language in a blog post referring to keeping dolphins in marine parks to entertain human visitors:

Positive – similar to humans

Suggests violent removal

Imprisonment

Contrast

Imprisoned

Strong words suggesting that dolphins are sensitive

Unnatural, restricted chemical

Positive – makes them sound like humans

Many of the highly intelligent and social animals incarcerated in marine parks around the world have endured the trauma of being caught and torn away from their families in the wild and then sold into a life of captivity. In the wild, dolphins swim together in family pods for their entire lives. In the chlorinated prisons of marine parks, their ocean worlds are reduced to claustrophobic swimming pools. Most captive dolphins die prematurely, living to only half the age of their wild brothers and sisters.

from Anne's blog on PETA website (http://blog.peta.org.uk)

1 Write one or more paragraphs from an animal lover's point of view on one of the following:

- Zoos are just prisons for animals.
- Hunting animals or birds for 'fun' is uncivilised.
- Eating meat is wrong.
- Bull-fighting should be banned.

Copy some of the techniques of the PETA blog post, using emotive language – negative and positive.

# Rhetorical techniques

There are a number of language techniques used to persuade, known as **rhetorical techniques**.

## ACTIVITY 2

Here is a typical exam task:

*Write a letter to the editor of a national newspaper, protesting against the building of new roads across the countryside.*

Read the following extract, in which a Grade 5 student presents his views. Notice how he uses rhetorical devices.

Emotive verb choice

Pair of similar words, with 'un-f' repetition

The road they are wanting to build near where I live should be stopped. If this unaffordable and unforgiveable road is built it will rip a village in half, ruin a river valley, and create a path of death for wildlife. The sound of birdsong will be drowned out by howling speeding lorries. And before that, there will be months of noise, disruption, delays and pollution.
    Planners claim we need a fast link between Brentford and Dartwell, but we know there is a perfectly good road already. Planners claim that the road will create jobs, but we know that will only be while it's being built. Planners claim that some needs come before those of local residents, but we know why: none of the planners live locally.
    Everywhere we look, cars and concrete are taking over from fields and forests. Wildlife is smashed by the hammer of big money. Why must we bow down to progress?

Metaphor

Metaphor; also a triple – the third bad thing in a row

List (of negative effects)

A triple statement; repeated sentence pattern – 'Planners claim ... but we know'

Alliteration emphasising opposite alternatives

Emotive metaphor

Rhetorical question

**1** Write at least one paragraph of a persuasive letter to the same newspaper, presenting a viewpoint which is in favour of this same new road. Try to use three of the rhetorical techniques used in the first letter. You could use positive language to describe the road and its effects, and negative language to describe those who oppose it.

One way to add persuasive power to your writing is to appeal directly to your reader – make it personal by using 'we', 'our', 'you' and 'your'.

Read these two extracts from Greenpeace's website. See how they appeal directly to the reader.

## Text A

*We are all responsible*

**About climate change: the causes**

As **we burn** up the planet's coal, oil and gas supplies and destroy vast areas of forests and peatlands, greenhouse gases are pouring into the atmosphere and disrupting the delicate balance of gases that sustains life on our planet. This is changing **our world** and having devastating impacts on people and environments.

*Shared ownership*

*We are all affected*

The overwhelming majority of climate scientists all agree on this – the rising global temperatures **we've recently experienced** are down to human activity.

Greenpeace

## Text B

**Get Active as an individual**

Greenpeace depends on the passion and enthusiasm of **people like you** to win campaigns and to create the change we need to see to build a green and peaceful world.

*What is the reader supposed to think when they read this?*

In the UK there are over 1000 Greenpeace active supporters, who organise themselves into local groups and networks. If there is a group / network near you then there are **loads of ways you can get involved, so please get in touch with your local coordinator.**

*Is this positive or negative? Explain.*

*If there is a 'local coordinator' why might this attract people?*

If however you can't join a Greenpeace local group / network, then don't worry. There are **plenty of things you can do** in your area as an individual, or with a couple of friends.

Greenpeace

*What is the intended effect here?*

**2** Write a persuasive article for your school magazine appealing to students to take part in a 24-hour sponsored fast to raise money to fight famine in Africa.

Write three paragraphs to present your point of view:

- Use the pronouns 'we' and 'they', and the possessives 'our' and 'their' to make readers feel how fortunate they are compared with many people in Africa; e.g. we have plenty to eat, and they do not.

- Use the pronoun 'you' and the possessive 'your' to tell readers *why* they should get involved.

- Tell readers *how* they can get involved – the **'call to action'** (signing up, getting sponsors, publicity, etc.).

**call to action** is the part of a persuasive appeal that tries to get the reader to do something – for example, donate money or join a protest

Read the following extract from a Grade 4 response to the task 'Write a student magazine article to put forward the view that young people should rely less on technology.'

> People nowadays rely so much on technology that they are forgetting basic skills. As they mess with their smartphones and mp3 players, they should ask themselves if they really need them. I often see two teenagers sitting next to each other, sending text messages to their friends. They don't think that they could talk to each other instead. They could also whistle or sing a song, instead of plugging in a set of earphones.

Rewrite this giving it more persuasive appeal by addressing the reader directly, in order to turn it into a Grade 5 response. Use some of the techniques used in the two Greenpeace webpage extracts.

# 4 Using evidence

In any kind of writing with a viewpoint, you will strengthen your case by providing evidence. One useful source of evidence is the exam paper itself – the two sources in Part A. You do not have to use these in your writing, but you may find it helpful to use some of their information.

## Practising for success

### ACTIVITY 1

1 Imagine you are given the following source in Section A of your exam. Make a list of the information you might use from it in an article giving your views on shoplifting.

**Examiner comment**

Use the information in Section A but don't simply copy it! Put ideas into your own words and if you are using facts and figures, put them into your own sentences.

It is a given that celebrities like to be in front of the cameras, but Antony Worrall Thompson could probably have done without the spotlight cast on him last week when he was filmed stealing wine and cheese from his local Tesco store in Henley-on-Thames.

Five times over the Christmas period the chef was caught by the store's security camera putting only some of his items through the self-service checkout machines, then walking out with the rest.

When confronted, '**Woz**' issued an **abject** apology. Why he stole the items, totalling £70.68, remains a mystery. On one occasion he paid £180 for three cases of champagne while stealing goods worth £4. His haul included bread and two tubs of discounted coleslaw.

If the incident exposed a man who seems to be having some sort of midlife crisis, it also focused attention on a very real retail crisis – the vast amount of money that shoplifting costs British stores and shoppers each year. Some £4.4 billion worth of goods was stolen from British shops last year and the number of shoplifting incidents seems to be on the rise.

**Woz** is a nickname for Antony Worrall Thompson

**abject** means very humble

Facts are hard to come by – so much of it is unreported and shops are reluctant to reveal the magnitude of their losses for fear of being seen as easy targets – but Britain seems to be Europe's shoplifting capital. The Global Retail Theft Barometer estimates that British retailers' losses add up to £70 for every man, woman and child in the country, compared with £65 in France and £50 in Germany.

Despite spending more than £1 billion a year on cameras, guards, electronic tags and other security devices, British shops are engaged in a **war of attrition** against shoplifters, who range from professional steal-to-order criminals who make off with as much as £1,000 worth of goods a day, to bored teenagers to … middle-aged chefs.

Margaret Driscoll, *The Sunday Times* (2012)

a **war of attrition** is a campaign to wear down or reduce an enemy or problem

**2** Read this extract from a Grade 5 article making the point that shoplifting is not a serious crime. Jot down the key evidence it uses.

Of course, if £4.4 billion worth of goods were shoplifted in the UK in 2011, that is a lot. But I imagine businesses spend more than that on advertising. Also, if shops lose £70 per person through this crime, we know that we will all be paying at least that much in the increased prices we pay for what we buy, to compensate them.

Shoplifting matters but is only part of the problem. For a start, why do people steal from shops? If a rich TV celebrity chef like Antony Worrall Thompson steals £4 worth of food while actually paying £180 for champagne, this suggests that he is mentally disturbed, not just a simple criminal. And if teenagers from poor families steal from shops, is that partly because advertising makes them feel hard done by?

I personally have friends who have stolen from shops. In one case this was because she felt under pressure because of bullying. In another, a boy was trying to impress his big brother. I know that was wrong, but it was not as simple as just being greedy.

**Examiner comment**

An anecdote (personal story) counts as evidence, even if you make it up. It is not the kind of 'evidence' that would be accepted in court, but it can add weight to your exam response.

**Discussion point**

**3** Discuss how this response does the following:
   **a)** adapts information instead of just copying it
   **b)** interprets information to make relevant points
   **c)** adds to the information with personal evidence.
   Decide if there is an anecdote you would have added.

**Boost your grade**

**1** Read this Grade 3 student extract and discuss:
- how well evidence has been used
- how the ideas could be put differently to make the argument clearer
- what else could have been added in this section.

> My friend Chris stole a sweatshirt from a store just to show off. The celebrity chef stole very expensive champagne when he did not need to. Shop-lifting is very serious in Britain and comes to billions of £££ every year. Shops lose £70 for everyone in the country in a year. For these reasons I think that it should be treated much more seriously. Tough sentences would do a lot to stop people doing it. People say it doesn't actually hurt anybody, but we all have to pay for it.

**2** Keeping the same basic ideas, rewrite the extract to earn a higher grade. You can make up information or use different details from the *Sunday Times* exam text if you wish.

## Test yourself

Write an article for a youth magazine explaining your views on what you think Britain will be like in twenty years' time and why it will be like that.

- Focus in detail on just four or five features.
- Plan your article, especially your opening – to grab the reader's attention – and conclusion – to round off your viewpoint.
- Consider how you will interest your readers.
- Use a range of techniques.
- Vary sentence lengths and types.
- Try to use a range of vocabulary and punctuation.

When you have 'finished', read through what you have written and correct the errors and improve the expression.

**Examiner comment**

Very few students check their work carefully. However, when the quality has been improved, the grade will be higher!

**What you have learned**

In this unit you have learned how to:
- assess different types of writing task
- explain your point of view and why you hold it
- argue a case logically
- write to persuade, using emotive and rhetorical language
- use different types of evidence.

# CREDITS AND ACKNOWLEDGEMENTS

## Photo credits

**p.2** © ead72 – Fotolia; **p.6** © Photodisc/Getty Images; **p.8** © Jamie Mann/ Alamy; **p.9** © Botterill/Getty Images; **p.11** STONE COLD by Robert Swindells (Puffin, 2005). Cover reproduced with permission from Penguin Books Ltd.; **p.12** c.20thC.Fox/Everett/Rex Features; **p.13** © Yuri Kravchenko – Fotolia; **p.15** © Bain News Service/Buyenlarge/Getty Images; **p.16 top** © shaiith – Fotolia; **bottom** ©TopFoto; **p.19** © Mike Hewitt/ALLSPORT/Getty Images; **p.25** © Roger-Viollet/TopFoto; **p.27** © CCat82 – Fotolia; **p.30** © snaptitude – Fotolia; **p.37** © Moviestore Collection/REX; **p.40** Cover of 'Shadow of the Wind' by Carlos Ruiz Zafón, published by The Orion Publishing Group; **p.45** © mariusz szczygieł – Fotolia.com; **p.46** © kichigin19 – Fotolia.com; **p.47** © Stephen Meese – Fotolia.com; **p.48** © Tihon RF/Alamy; **p.49** © Dreamworks/ Everett/REX; **pp.50–51** © Hulton-Deutsch Collection/CORBIS; **p.56** © yurkaimmortal – fotolia; **p.59** © Image Source/REX; **p.60** © wavebreakmedia/Shutterstock.com; **p.62** © Victoria and Albert Museum, London; **p.65** © Nickolay Khoroshkov – Fotolia; **p.68** © Library of Congress, LC-USZ62-5513; **p.70** © Martin Turzak – Fotolia; **p.72** © Wellcome Library/Creative Commons CC BY 4.0 http:// creativecommons.org/licenses/by/4.0; **p.73** © Wellcome Library/Creative Commons CC BY 4.0 http://creativecommons.org/licenses/by/4.0; **p.74** © Pics money – Fotolia; **p.76** © Wellcome Library/Creative Commons CC BY 4.0 http://creativecommons.org/licenses/by/4.0; **p.77** © National Pictures/TopFoto; **p.78** © Getty Images/Gallo Images; **p.80** © Popperfoto/ Getty Images; **p.82** © Library of Congress Prints & Photographs_LC-DIG-ppmsca-19926; **p.86** Public domain/http://commons.wikimedia.org/ wiki/File:Winston_Churchill_during_the_General_Election_Campaign_ in_1945_HU55965.jpg; **p.87** © Broadimage/Rex Features; **p.88** © Don Arnold/WireImage/Getty Images; **p.90** © Snap/Rex Features; **p.93** © by Archive Photos/Getty Images; **p.94** © nyul – Fotolia; **p.96** public domain/ http://commons.wikimedia.org/wiki/File:Bell_box_telephone_with_ thumper_1877.jpg; **p.97** © Illustrated London News; **p.99** ©TopFoto; **p.106** © Monkey Business Images/Shutterstock.com; **p.108** © Tamara Kulikova – Fotolia; **p.110** © Ror – Fotolia; **p.114** © Kevin Mazur/ KCSports2014/Getty Images; **p.116** © Dariusz Gora/Shutterstock.com; **p.118** © Joseph Helfenberger – Fotolia; **p.119** © Chris Mole/Shutterstock. com; **p.122** © JackF – Fotolia; **p.123** © Eric Gevaert – Fotolia; **p.125** © Billy Stock/Robert Harding/REX Features; **p.127** © Jonathan Hordle/ Rex Features; **p.128** Artwork © Published by arrangement with The Random House Group Limited; **p.130** © Getty Images/Blend Images; **p.132** © Tony Lee and Dan Boultwood; **p.133** © Walt Disney Co./Courtesy Everett/Rex Features; **p.140** © Picture Perfect/Rex Features; **p.142** © Phil Walter/Getty Images; **p.143** © Gamma-Keystone/Getty Images; **p.144** © Ferdaus Shamim/WireImage/Getty Images; **p.149** © Sipa Press/Rex Features; **p.150** © Liverpool FC via Getty Images; **p.152** © Vendigo – Fotolia; **p.154** © jennyt/Shutterstock.com; **p.155** © Public Domain/ http://commons.wikimedia.org/wiki/File:Marley%27s_Ghost_-_A_ Christmas_Carol_(1843),_opposite_25_-_BL.jpg; **p.158** © Gonzales Photo/ Malthe Ivarss/ Rex Features; **p.163** © tommaso79/Shutterstock.com; **p.164** © H. Armstrong Roberts/ClassicStock/Topfoto; **p.168** © Jake Lyell/ Alamy; **p.169** © Universal History Archive/ Universal Images Group/Rex Features; **p.171** © d0r0thy – fotolia; **p.177** © Kzenon – Fotolia; **p.178** © Pablo Porciuncula/AFP/Getty Images; **p.182** © Francois Gohier/TopFoto; **p.183** © Roy Pedersen/Shutterstock.com; **p.184** © Jose Jordan/AFP/Getty Images; **p.185** © Jürgen Fälchle – Fotolia; **p.186** © Lisa S./Shutterstock.com

## Acknowledgements

**p.3: Doris Lessing:** From 'Through the Tunnel' from *Through the Tunnel – Tale Blazers* (Perfection Learning, 1989); **p.5: Robert Swindells:** from *Daz 4 Zoe* (Puffin, 1995), © Robert Swindells. Reproduced by permission of the publisher; Robert Swindells: Extract (120 words) from *Daz 4 Zoe* (Puffin, 1995), **p.6: Ray Bradbury:** From 'The Fog Horn' from *The Golden Apples of the Sun* (Avon Books, 2008); **p.7: Lloyd Jones:** from *Mister Pip* (John Murray, 2008); **p.7: Lloyd Jones:** from *Mister Pip* (John Murray, 2008), © Lloyd Jones. Reproduced by permission of the publisher; **p.8: Nick Hornby:** from *Fever Pitch* (Penguin, 2010); **p.8: Nick Hornby:** from *Fever Pitch* (Penguin, 2010), © Nick Hornby. Reproduced by permission of the publisher; **p.10: Chinua Achebe:** from *Things Fall Apart* (Penguin, 2006); **p.10: Chinua Achebe:** from *Things Fall Apart* (Penguin, 2006), © Chinua Achebe. Reproduced by permission of the publisher; **p.11: Robert Swindells:** from *Stone Cold* (Puffin, 1995), © Robert Swindells. Reproduced by permission of the publisher and the Jennifer Luithlen Agency; Robert Swindells: Extract (170 words) from *Stone Cold* (Puffin, 1995); **pp.11–12: Yann Martel:** from *The Life of Pi* (Canongate Books, 2012); **pp.13,14–15: Michael Morpurgo:** from *War Horse* (Egmont, 2007), from *War Horse* by Michael Morpurgo. Text copyright © 1982 Michael Morpurgo. Published by Egmont UK Ltd London and used with permission; **p.18: Robert Swindells:** from *Brother in the Land* (Puffin, 1994); extract from *Brother in the Land* by Robert Swindells (OUP, 1998) copyright © Robert Swindells 1984, reprinted by permission of Oxford University Press; **p.19: Ian McEwan:** from *Enduring Love* (Vintage, 1998), © Ian McEwan. Reproduced by permission of the publisher; **p.19: Ian McEwan:** from *Enduring Love* (Vintage, 1998); **pp.20,35: Michael Grant:** from *Gone* (Electric Monkey, 2010), from *Gone* by Michael Grant. Text copyright © 2008 Michael Grant. Published by Egmont UK Ltd London and used with permission; **pp.20–21: Sue Limb:** from *Girl, (Nearly) 16, Absolute Torture* (Bloomsbury, 2010), **p.23: Donna Kauffman:** from *Sugar Rush* (Brava, 2012), © Donna Kauffman. Reproduced by permission of the publisher; **p.26: Narinder Dhami:** from *Bend it Like Beckham* (Hodder, 2002), © Narinder Dhami. Reproduced by permission of the publisher; **p.26: Narinder Dhami:** from *Bend it Like Beckham* (Hodder, 2002); **pp.27,173: Meera Syal:** from *Anita and Me* (Flamingo, 1997); **pp.28–29: Mark Haddon:** from *The Curious Incident of the Dog in the Night-Time* (Vintage, 2004), © Mark Haddon. Reproduced by permission of the publisher; **pp.28–29: Mark Haddon:** from *The Curious Incident of the Dog in the Night-Time* (Vintage, 2004); **p.30: Jennifer Donnelly:** from *A Gathering Light* (Bloomsbury, 2004); **p.30: Jennifer Donnelly:** from *A Gathering Light* (Bloomsbury, 2004); **p.30: Jennifer Donnelly:** from *A Gathering Light* (Bloomsbury, 2004), excerpt from *A Northern Light* by Jennifer Donnelly. Copyright (c) 2003 by Jennifer Donnelly. Reprinted by permission of Houghton Mifflin Harcourt Publishing Company. All rights reserved; **p.31: Rachel Hawkins:** from *Hex Hall* (Simon and Schuster, 2010); **p.32: Charles Higson:** from *The Enemy* (Puffin, 2010), © Charles Higson. Reproduced by permission of Disney Publishing Worldwide and Penguin UK; **p.33: Katie Dale:** from *Someone Else's Life* (Simon and Schuster, 2012); **p.34: Michael Frayn:** from *Spies* (Faber & Faber, 2011); **p.37: Steig Larsson:** from *The Girl with the Dragon Tattoo* (Quercus, 2008), © Steig Larsson. Reproduced by permission of the publisher; Carlos Ruiz Zafón: Extract (425 words) from *The Shadow of the Wind* (Phoenix, 2005); **p.39: Carlos Ruiz Zafón:** from *The Shadow of the Wind* (Phoenix, 2005), © Carlos Ruiz Zafón. Reproduced by permission of the publisher; **p.39: Carlos Ruiz Zafón:** from *The Shadow of the Wind* (Phoenix, 2005); **p.41: Annabel Pitcher:** from *Ketchup Clouds* (Indigo,

2012); **p.42: William Golding:** from *Lord of the Flies* (Faber & Faber, 1997); **pp.44–45,46: Annabel Pitcher:** from *My Sister Lives on the Mantelpiece* (Indigo, 2013); **p.48: Susan Hill:** from *I'm King of the Castle* (Penguin, 2014); **p.49: Khaled Hosseini:** from *The Kite Runner* (Bloomsbury, 2011); from *THE KITE RUNNER* by Khaled Hosseini, copyright © 2003 by Khaled Hosseini. Used by permission of the publisher and Riverhead Books, an imprint of Penguin Group (USA) LLC; **pp.50–51: Ben Elton:** from *The First Casualty* (Black Swan, 2006), © Ben Elton. Reproduced by permission of the publisher; **p.52: Roddy Doyle:** from *A Greyhound of a Girl* (Marion Lloyd Books, 2012); **p.53: Robert O'Brien:** from *Z is for Zachariah* (Puffin, 1998), © Robert O'Brien. Reproduced by permission of The Karpfinger Agency and Penguin UK. *Z is for Zachariah* by Robert O'Brien (Copyright © Robert O'Brien, 1976) Reprinted by permission of A.M. Heath & Co Ltd.; **p.53: Robert O'Brien:** from *Z is for Zachariah* (Puffin, 1998); **p.54: Barry Hines:** from *A Kestrel for a Knave* (Penguin, 2000), © Barry Hines. Reproduced by permission of the publisher and The Agency UK; **pp.55–56: Frank McCourt:** from *Angela's Ashes* (Harper Perennial, 2005); **p.59: Damian Carrington and George Arnett:** From 'Clear differences between organic and non-organic food, study finds' from *The Guardian* (*The Guardian*, 11th July 2014), copyright Guardian News & Media Ltd 2014, reproduced by permission of the publisher; **p.60: David Atkinson:** Based on 'Are fathers better at bedtime stories than mothers?' from *The Telegraph* (The Telegraph, 9th June 2014), © Telegraph Media Group Limited 2014, reproduced by permission of the publisher; **p.61: Leicester Mercury:** 'Richard III: Website details history of king found under Leicester car park', from Leicester Mercury (Leicester Mercury, 3rd February 2014); **pp.62,63: Author Unknown:** 'Cinema India: The Art of Bollywood' from The Victoria and Albert Museum website (The Victoria and Albert Museum, 2002), © Victoria and Albert Museum, London, http://www.vam.ac.uk/content/articles/c/cinema-india-the-art-of-bollywood/; **pp.64–65: Ma Jian:** From 'Red Dust' from *A taste of the best travel writing* (The Telegraph, 11th September 2002), © Telegraph Media Group Limited 2002, reproduced by permission of the publisher; **p.66: Salil Shetty:** From 'Now Stop It' from Amnesty UK Magazine, Issue 181 (Amnesty UK, Summer 2014); **p.67: Mike Harding:** From 'Enter an Egyptian Doctor covered in cat poo' from *Hypnotising the Cat* (Robson Books, 1998); **p.68: Mark Twain:** From 'Old Times on the Mississippi' from *Atlantic Monthly* (Atlantic Monthly, 1875); **p.70: Rachel Cooke:** From 'Enough of this anti-London bile. It will achieve nothing but harm' from *The Observer* (The Observer, 31st May 2014), copyright Guardian News & Media 2014, reproduced by permission of the publisher; **pp.71–72: Charles Olson:** Extract from 'The Receiving End' from *Penguin English Project Stage 2* (Penguin, 1973); **p.73: John Ruskin:** Extract from a lecture given at the Working Men's Institute in Camberwell (1865); **pp.74,124–125: Bill Bryson:** from *Notes from a Small Island* (Black Swan, 1996), © Bill Bryson. Reproduced by permission of the publisher; **p.76: Florence Nightingale:** Extract from a letter written in 1868 from Florence Nightingale on Public Healthcare, Lynn McDonald (Wilfrid Laurier University Press, 2004); **p.77: Olivia Rzadkiewicz:** From 'British nurse with Ebola virus has 'very good' chance of survival' from *The Telegraph* (The Telegraph, 26th August 2014), © Telegraph Media Group Limited 2014, reproduced by permission of the publisher; **p.78: Steve Rocliffe:** From 'A cycling tour of Cuba: readers' travel writing competition' from *The Guardian* (The Guardian, 6th September 2014), copyright Guardian News & Media Ltd 2014, reproduced by permission of the publisher; **p.80: Mo Farah:** from *Twin Ambitions* (Hodder & Stoughton, 2013); **p.82: Abraham Lincoln:** from *The Gettysburg address* (19th November 1863); **p.84: Beatrice Campbell:** Extract from a letter (18th November 1912); **p.86: Winston Churchill:** from *We Shall Fight on the Beaches* (4th June 1940); **p.87: Stuart Heritage:** From 'How to dodge the ice bucket challenge' from *The Guardian* (The Guardian, 26th August 2014), copyright Guardian News & Media Ltd 2014, reproduced by permission of the publisher; **pp.88–89: Hannah Ellis–Petersen:** From 'Bollywood superstar Shah Rukh Khan named world's second richest actor' from *The Guardian* (The Guardian, 21st May 2014), copyright Guardian News & Media Ltd 2014, reproduced by permission of the publisher; **p.93: Mrs C.E. Humphry:** from *Manners for Women* (1897); **p.94: Louisa Peacock:** From 'Women feel need to 'act like men' to get ahead at work' from *The Telegraph* (The Telegraph, 13th September 2013), © Telegraph Media Group Limited 2013, reproduced by permission of the publisher; **pp.96–97: The New York Times:** From 'Dr. Bell, Inventor of Telephone, Dies' from *On This Day August 3, 1922* (The New York Times, 2010), www.nytimes.com; **p.97: Author Unknown:** from Alexander Graham Bell Biography (www.biography.com, 3rd November 2014); **p.99: Telegraph View:** From 'Remembering sacrifices of the past – and present' from *The Telegraph* (The Telegraph, 11th July 2014), © Telegraph Media Group Limited 2014, reproduced by permission of the publisher; **pp.100–101: Captain George Vernon Clarke:** From a letter (1899); **p.103: Judith Kerr:** from *The Tiger who came to Tea* (HarperCollins, 2006); **p.104: Author Unknown:** from Top of the Pops Magazine (Immediate Media, November 2014); ©Immediate Media Co London Ltd 2014; **p.107: R.J. Palacio:** from *Wonder* (Corgi Childrens, 2013); **p.107: R.J. Palacio:** from *Wonder* (Corgi Childrens, 2013), © R.J. Palacio. Reproduced by permission of the publisher; **p.107: Gillian Cross:** from *Tightrope* (OUP, 2010), extract from *Tightrope* by Gillian Cross (OUP, 2010), copyright © Gillian Cross 1999, reprinted by permission of Oxford University Press; **p.109: Kevin Brooks:** from *The Bunker Diary* (Penguin, 2013), © Kevin Brooks. Reproduced by permission of the publisher; **p.109: Charlie Brooker:** from *The Hell of it All* (Faber & Faber, 2012); **p.114: Mark Edmonds:** From 'A Life in the Day: I never think of myself as any different from anyone else' from *The Sunday Times* (The Sunday Times, 2nd February 2014), copyright News International 2014, reproduced by permission of the publisher; **p.116: Ally Kennen:** from *Berserk* (Marion Lloyd Books, 2010); **p.118: Author Unknown:** From 'Calvin Harris Biography' from Ace Showbiz (www.aceshowbiz.com); **p.121: Stephen King:** from *The Dark Tower: The Waste Lands* (Hodder, 2012); **p.120: Darren Shan:** from *Bec* (HarperCollins, 2013); **p.122: Alfred, Lord Tennyson:** from 'The Eagle' (1851); **p.128: Malorie Blackman:** from *Noughts and Crosses* (Corgi Childrens, 2006), © Malorie Blackman. Reproduced by permission of the publisher; **p.132: Tony Lee and Dan Boultwood:** from *Sherlock Holmes The Baker Street Irregulars: The adventure of the missing detective* (Franklin Watts, 2011); **p.133: Walt Disney Animation Studios:** Adapted from 'Big Hero 6 summary' (Walt Disney Animation Studios, 2014); **p.133: Ben Child:** From 'Big Hero 6 marks Disney's first proper step into comic-book adaptation' from *The Guardian* (The Guardian, 2nd September 2014), copyright Guardian News & Media Ltd 2014, reproduced by permission of the publisher; **p.142: Marc Heywood:** Extract from Jim Telfer's 1997 speech. From 'The Power of Speech' from www.lionsrugby.com (Lions Rugby, 2nd July 2013); **p.143: Fatima Meer:** From Nelson Mandela's 'An ideal for which I am prepared to die' from *Higher than Hope: A Biography of Nelson Mandela* (Penguin, 1990); **pp.144–145: Michael Palin:** from *Himalaya* (Weidenfeld & Nicolson, 2004), © Michael Palin. Reproduced by permission of the publisher; **pp.144–145: Michael Palin:** from *Himalaya* (Weidenfeld & Nicolson, 2004), HIMALAYA © 2005 by Michael Palin. Reprinted by permission of St. Martin's Press and Weidenfeld & Nicolson. All rights reserved; **p.146: Veronica Roth:** from *Divergent* (HarperCollins, 2014); **p.152: Ernest Shackleton:** from *South: the endurance expedition* (Penguin, 2013); **p.155: Charles Dickens:** from *A Christmas Carol* (1843); **pp.164,167,168: Ernest Hemingway:** 'The Short Happy Life of Francis Macomber' from The Essential Hemingway (Arrow, 1995); **p.165: David Lodge:** From 'Hotel des Boobs' from *The Penguin Book of Modern British Short Stories* (Penguin, 2011); **p.165: Truman Capote:** from *Children on their birthdays* (Penguin, 2011); **p.165: F. Scott Fitzgerald:** from *Basil: The Freshest Boy* (1928); **p.169: W.W. Jacobs:** from *The Monkey's Paw* (1902); **p.172: Ken Kesey:** from One Flew over the Cuckoo's Nest (Penguin, 2005); **p.172: Ken Kesey:** from *One Flew over the Cuckoo's Nest* (Penguin, 2005), © Ken Kesey. Reproduced by permission of the publisher; **pp.176–177: Carol Midgley:** From 'Bad behaviour in the supermarket doesn't leave me rolling in the aisles' from *The Times* (The Times, 5th March 2009), copyright News International 2009, reproduced by permission of the publisher; **p.182: Anne Clark:** From 'Simon Cowell Axes 'Xtra Factor' Dolphin Scenes' from PETA (http://blog.peta.org.uk, 30th September 2014), © PETA. Reproduced with permission. www.peta.org.uk; **p.184: Author Unknown:** From 'About climate change' from Greenpeace (Greenpeace UK, 4th September 2013), © Greenpeace. Reproduced with permission. www.greenpeace.org.uk; **p.184: Author Unknown:** From 'Get Active as an individual from Greenpeace (Greenpeace UK, 18th October 2012), © Greenpeace. Reproduced with permission. www.greenpeace.org.uk; **pp.185–186: Margarette Driscoll:** From 'Oh no, we're not shoplifting, just "liberating"' from *The Sunday Times* (The Sunday Times, 15th January 2012), copyright News International 2012, reproduced by permission of the publisher.